CONTENTS

100 GREATEST BATTLES

ANGUS KONSTAM

OSPREY
PUBLISHING

INTRODUCTION

This book deals with the battles which changed history. Some were spectacular and decisive military victories, while others altered the course of a hard-fought conflict. Others had a longer-term impact, through technological innovation, or by their economic or political ramifications. One person's idea of what qualifies as a 'greatest battle' may be different from someone else's; it is a subjective choice drawing on the person's own historical perceptions. That can involve anything from their own national perspective, their own enthusiasm for certain historical periods over others, and even their own personal stake in the past. For instance, when I served in the military, I was a sailor rather than a soldier, and so it is inevitable that battles like Trafalgar, Jutland and Midway make the list.

This said, it is important to make sure the prefix 'greatest' is fully earned. The main arbiter is to ensure that the battle I've included was significant enough to change the course of a war or a campaign. Its outcome had a profound effect on what followed, or at least marked a major turning point in a conflict. For example, Stalingrad itself didn't end World War II, but it marked a clearly definable turning point in it. A few saw the development of new tactics, or the first major use of new technology. Others are included because of the importance they have in the shaping of the nations that make up the modern world.

Unfortunately, war has been a key feature of mankind's existence ever since the dawn of prehistory. For the battles to make the list, though, they needed to be well-enough documented that they could be described in reasonable detail. The list begins, then, when historians began leaving a written record of these key past events. Obviously, weaponry has changed over the centuries, as have tactics, and the way troops were deployed on the battlefield. What hasn't changed, though, is the fundamental objective of warfare. The constant theme running from first battle to last is the use of warfare as a means of shaping the world we live in.

Almost all of the battles included here have been covered in Osprey's superb Campaign series, by authors with a specialist knowledge of that particular era, campaign or battle. So, I was able to draw upon their knowledge, and thus I remain greatly in their debt. As a historian, I recognize that fallibility in any history book is almost impossible to avoid. I hope that these instances are minimal, but, where they do arise, these are entirely of my own doing. That said, I hope you enjoy this 2,000-year journey through human conflict, and if this book helps cast even a little light on this great arc of history, then it has served its purpose.

Angus Konstam
Herston, Orkney 2023

THE ANCIENT WORLD

MARATHON, 10 SEPTEMBER 490 BC

In 499 BC, the independent-minded Greek cities in Asia Minor rose up in revolt against the Persian Empire, which governed them with a heavy hand. This marked the start of half a century of intermittent conflict between Persia and the Greek city states. It took six years to quell the uprising, but the Persian ruler, King Darius 'the Great', vowed to punish Athens and other city states which had supported the rebels. In 492 BC the Persians subjugated Thrace and Macedon, and two years later they did the same to the Aegean islands. It was then that Darius turned his attention to Athens. So began the first Greek and Persian War – a struggle for regional supremacy by one side and a fight for freedom by the other.

In the summer of 490 BC the Persians conquered the island state of Euboea, which lay close to Attica on the Greek mainland. It was inevitable that Athens would be Darius' next target, and so the Athenians requested support from the other Greek states. Before most of these could gather, though, the Persian army landed on the Attican coast near the town of Marathon. Marathon lay on the edge of a small coastal plain, which had become a sprawling Persian encampment. The Athenian general Miltiades managed to occupy the high ground bordering the plain. This meant the Persians were forced to deploy for battle on the crowded plain, where they lacked the room to make full use of their superior numbers.

Although the sources, including Herodotus, are vague about the size of the two armies, it is generally assumed that Miltiades commanded around 10,000 troops, most of whom were hoplites – the well-trained armoured spearmen favoured by the Greeks. The Persian commander Datis had roughly 25,000 men, most of whom were archers and spearmen. Some of these, though, were still embarked on the Persian fleet. The two armies confronted each other for five days before either commander made his move. Then, on 10 September, battle began when

Miltiades ordered a general advance. His hoplites closed rapidly, to reduce casualties from Persian arrows. Then the two lines clashed.

The battle was a bloody, close-quarter affair, and the Greeks fought well. Eventually, however, their centre was pushed back. This was the moment of crisis for Miltiades. Fortunately his flanks had held firm, and the Persians in the centre found themselves outflanked. Eventually they broke and ran towards their ships, at which point the rest of the Persian army joined the rout. The Athenians pursued them, hacking down the Persians as they tried to reach the safety of their fleet.

According to Herodotus some 5,000 Persians were killed in the battle, while the Greeks lost less than 200 men. Once the remnants of his army were safely aboard, Datis led the Persian fleet to Athens, hoping to capture the city before the Athenian army returned. Miltiades, though, had force-marched his men back to the city, and Datis was thwarted. The Persians would return, however, and in even greater numbers. Allegedly a runner was sent to Athens with news of the victory, an achievement which led to the sporting 'marathon' of today, where modern runners cover the same approximate distance between Marathon and Athens.

LEFT The charge of the Athenian hoplites should have decided the battle, but the Persians stubbornly held their ground, and in the centre the attackers were even driven back. Eventually, though, the superior training of the hoplites turned the tide, and the Persian line was broken. (Richard Hook © Osprey Publishing)

THERMOPYLAE, LATE AUGUST 480 BC

In 486 BC, the Persian King Darius died and was succeeded by his son Xerxes. He spent six years planning to avenge Persia's defeat at Marathon, amassing an army of up to 200,000 men. He finally made his move in the spring of 480 BC, crossing the Hellespont which divided Europe and Asia Minor. His host marched through Thrace, Macedonia and Thessaly, while the Persian fleet kept pace with it, supplying the army as it marched south along the coast.

The Greek city states were divided, as many chose to submit to King Xerxes, or to stay neutral. Athens and Sparta, though, led the Greek alliance which opposed the Persian invasion. It would take time for this Greek army to assemble, and so, to buy time, King Leonidas

of Sparta led a small Greek allied force to Thermopylae.

Here, to the south of Thessaly, the narrow coastal plain which led to Lokris, Boetia and Attica was constricted by the mountains, forming a narrow pass. With the Persians approaching, Leonidas decided to make a stand there, to gain time for the rest of Greece to rally. He had 7,000 men at his command, including 300 Spartans. Xerxes' army vastly outnumbered the Greek defenders, but they were prevented from overwhelming the Greeks due to the narrowness of the pass. It was only around 300 metres wide at its narrowest point, where an old defensive wall spanned the coastal road. Xerxes realized he had to break through, nevertheless, as unless it reached the fertile lands further south, his army would quickly run out of food.

Xerxes' first frontal assault by 10,000 Medes was preceded by a massed storm of arrows, but it had little effect. The attackers were repulsed with heavy losses. Xerxes then sent in his elite infantry, the 'Immortals', which met the same fate. Greek losses had been minimal. The battle ended before nightfall, but the following morning Xerxes launched another attack. This too was beaten back. It was then that Xerxes' luck changed. A local man, Ephialtes of Thrachis, was brought to the king, and told him there was a pass through the mountains which would emerge behind the Greeks. That evening, the Persian general Hydarnes led a force of 20,000 Immortals along the path, and by dawn they had emerged on the coastal plain. A rearguard of Phoenician hoplites was brushed aside, and Hydarnes advanced on the rear of Leonidas' small army.

When they learned of this, many of the Greeks withdrew, but Leonidas and his 300 Spartans, plus up to 1,100 other Greeks elected to fight to the death. Assailed from both front and rear, their fate was inevitable. After Leonidas was killed, the survivors made a last stand on a small hill, but they were eventually cut down. The sacrifice of Leonidas and his 300 Spartans has become a symbol of heroism in the face of overwhelming odds. It also helped to unite the Greeks, which would eventually lead to the defeat of Xerxes and his army.

LEFT At Thermopylae, the end came once the Persians found a way to outflank the Spartan defences. Then, attacked from all sides, the end was inevitable. Here, the bareheaded Spartan King Leonidas falls, sword in hand, as his bodyguard fight on to the death. (Steve Noon © Osprey Publishing)

SALAMIS, SEPTEMBER 480 BC

As a result of the Persian victory at Thermopylae, Xerxes' army was free to conquer all of central Greece. As Xerxes ravaged Boetia and Attica, the bulk of the Greek army withdrew to the narrow Isthmus of Corinth, which they fortified. That meant that for the moment southern Greece was safe. A small detachment remained to defend Athens, but they were unable to prevent the Persians from scaling its walls and capturing the city. Most of the population had already fled, but Xerxes ordered Athens to be burned to the ground. Meanwhile the Persian fleet had been battered by storms in the Aegean, and then defeated in a naval clash off Artemisium. But it was still a powerful force of around 700 ships, and it rounded Attica to appear off Athens.

The smaller Greek allied fleet of 373 ships had gathered behind the nearby island of Salamis, and so battle was inevitable. Given his advantage in numbers, Xerxes was keen to fight. So too, though, was the Greek commander, the Spartan admiral Eurybiades. Half of his fleet was Athenian, and the rest was made up of contingents from other city states, including Corinth and Sparta. Most of the ships in the battle were 'triremes' – sleek galleys with three banks of oars. While marines were carried to fight boarding actions, their primary weapon was the ram. The two fleets remained inactive for up to two weeks as the Persians consolidated their control over Athens, then Xerxes ordered his fleet to row into the Strait of Salamis, in an attempt to bring the Greeks to battle. The Persian king's fleet was commanded jointly by his brothers Ariabagnes and Achaimines, and a favoured nobleman, Pexaspes.

Expecting a battle the next morning, Xerxes had his throne set up on Mount Egalio overlooking the Strait. After some debate that evening, the Greeks decided to fight. The next morning the Greeks formed their fleet up and advanced on the Persians. Then they stopped, which the Persians took as a sign of fear. Instead it was probably the Greeks concentrating their ships before attacking the less well-ordered Persian fleet. Then, on Eurybiades' command, the Greeks advanced. They smashed into the Persian front line, sinking numerous triremes, and driving the rest back into the lines behind them. The Persians became disordered, and Eurybiades unleashed his reserves, whose advance split the Persian fleet in two. The survivors then broke, either escaping out to sea or running aground. Ariabagnes was killed in the first assault. In all, around 300 Persians ships were lost in the battle compared with around 40 Greek ships. With his fleet defeated, Xerxes withdrew north into Thessaly to protect his supply lines. The war would continue, but after Salamis it was the Greeks who held the initiative, and control of the sea. Reinvigorated, they would go on to drive the Persians from Greek soil.

LEFT The naval clash at Salamis was watched from the shore by the Persian king Xerxes. Below him, the Persian galleys put to sea to confront the Greek fleet which appeared shortly after dawn, putting off from the island of Salamis and forming up in the Strait, facing their opponents. (Peter Dennis © Osprey Publishing)

PLATAEA, AUGUST 479 BC

In 480 BC, during the Second Persian invasion of Greece, the immense invading army led by King Xerxes I had defeated the Greeks at Thermopylae, and then ravaged the cities of Boetia and Attica, including Athens and Thebes. The smaller Greek allied army, though, remained behind a line of fortifications spanning the Isthmus of Corinth, and Xerxes was unable to bring them to battle. Then, the Persian fleet was roundly defeated in the Battle of Salamis, fought near Athens' port of Piraeus. Xerxes relied on his fleet to supply his army, and so this forced him to withdraw northwards into Thessaly. Having captured Athens and conquered much of Greece, the Persian king returned to Asia Minor for the winter, taking part of his army with him.

His senior general Mardonius was duly left in command of the remaining troops, and was tasked with completing the conquest of Greece the following year. However, the Greeks spent the winter gathering more troops, and by the spring they were able to field the largest allied army their city states had ever put into the field.

Although peace talks took place during the winter, with Mardonius' primary aim being to sever the Greek alliance, these talks came to nothing. Thus, when spring came and the Persians marched south into Attica, the Greek army abandoned its defensive position at Corinth and advanced northwards. Mardonius withdrew into Boetia and built a fortified camp near the city of Plataea to protect his infantry. The open ground around it was also perfectly suited to the Persian cavalry, and he was well supplied. It was clear to the Greeks that this position was virtually impregnable. During early August the armies faced each other, with the Greeks deployed on high ground overlooking the camp. Mardonius' agents spent the time sowing dissent among the Greeks, and his cavalry raided the Greek lines.

It was the Persian cavalry's capture of the Greeks' water supply that broke the stalemate.

This forced the Greeks to withdraw under cover of darkness, but this was badly handled, and at dawn the Greek army lay scattered and vulnerable. Mardonius immediately advanced out of his camp and gave battle. However, the Spartan rearguard was ready for them and held off the attackers, buying time for the other Greek contingents to join them. There were probably 80,000 Persian infantry on the field that day, and 5,000 cavalry, while the Greeks mustered around half that number, with much fewer cavalry. The Persian total also included some Greeks, most notably a Theban contingent. The Greek hoplites, though, were better trained and armoured. As more Greeks arrived to reinforce the Spartans the Persian Foot began to be driven back towards their camp. Then, when the Spartans killed Mardonius, the Persians began to flee. The Greeks pursued, trapping thousands of the invaders in their camp. After being pushed back by the Athenians the Thebans withdrew, leaving the Persians to their fate. The Greek victory was total – as much as three-quarters of the Persian army were cut down, for the loss of no more than 1,500 Greeks. The remnants of the Persian army retreated to Asia Minor, leaving the Greek city states free to govern themselves. But with the Persian threat gone, rather than remain united, the Greeks were more ready to fight amongst themselves.

LEFT When the Greeks attacked, the Persian infantry hoped to stem their advance. Here, the Persian commander Mardonius exhorts his men to fight harder, but they were unable to hold their ground against the better-armoured hoplites. When Mardonius was killed, resistance quickly crumbled. (Peter Dennis © Osprey Publishing)

LEUCTRA, 6 JULY 371 BC

After the Persian threat receded, Greek unity was short-lived. Athens became the dominant power in Greece, which incurred the enmity of its neighbours. Chief amongst these was Sparta, and a clash for supremacy between the two became inevitable. Although Sparta had emerged victorious in the hard-fought Peloponnesian War (431–404 BC) and had become the dominant Greek power, tensions remained high in the Greek world. The inconclusive Corinthian War (395–387 BC) saw Thebes, Athens and Corinth unite to oppose what amounted to Spartan imperialism, and Athens was able to regain some of its former power. Although a peace treaty was brokered, it was clear that the two sides still had scores to settle.

In 378 BC, when Sparta broke the terms of the treaty, Thebes ousted its pro-Spartan elements, and rose against it. The resulting Boetian War (378–371 BC) saw Thebes and its Boetian allies as well as Athens ranged against Sparta and the Peloponnesian League. Over the next few years punitive Spartan invasions of Boetia were repulsed, but the region was devastated. This, though, only served to strengthen anti-Spartan resolve. A temporary peace followed, but in the year 371 BC, the Spartan king Cleombrotus led a new army north to deal with Thebes. He commanded around 10,000 hoplites, and another 1,000 cavalry. This small but potent force captured the Boetian fortress of Creusis on the Gulf of Corinth, which Cleombrotus used as his forward base. From there he advanced through the hills towards Thebes.

At Leuctra the Spartans found the slightly smaller Boetian League's army arrayed for battle. Confident in the superiority of his Spartans, Cleombrotus decided to attack. The battle began with a clash between the rival light infantry and cavalry, with the Theban cavalry eventually driving their rivals from the field. This thwarted Cleombrotus' attempt to outflank the Theban left flank using his less experienced Peloponnesian

allies. Epaminondas, the Theban general who commanded the Boetians, had watched the enemy's approach. He countered by launching his own attack. His hoplite phalanxes advanced in echelon, with the elite Theban Sacred Band on the Boetian allies' left flank. Unusually, they were arrayed in a much deeper formation than the Spartan hoplite phalanx which faced them.

In the brutal clash that followed, the deeper Theban formation triumphed and broke the Spartan right-hand phalanx. The dead included King Cleombrotus. The other Boetian phalanxes had still to engage the Spartans when the Spartan right broke. Although the remaining Spartans fought on, their Peloponnesian allies withdrew from the fight, and the Boetian League's victory was complete. As well as their king, the Spartans lost at least 1,000 men in the battle – many of them their elite hoplites. The Thebans lost around 300 men, although again it was their elite Sacred Band which bore the brunt of the fight. The Theban victory at Leuctra broke Sparta's dominance in Greece, an achievement underlined by a second victory at Mantinea nine years later. Thebes became the dominant power in Greece, until the rise of Macedonia three decades later saw the end of the independent Greek city states.

LEFT The climax of the battle came when the Spartan phalanx was charged by their Theban opponents, spearheaded by the elite Sacred Band, all carrying their distinctive Herculean club shields. The better-disciplined Thebans eventually overpowered their less motivated Spartan counterparts. (Seán Ó'Brógáin © Osprey Publishing)

THE GRANICUS, MAY 334 BC

In the mid-4th century BC, King Philip II of Macedonia took advantage of the political disarray in Greece to expand the frontiers of his northern Greek realm. The Greek city states of Athens and Thebes opposed this expansion, but King Philip defeated them both at the Battle of Chaeronea. As a result, Philip became the unquestioned master of Greece. He planned to follow this with an invasion of Persia, but he was assassinated in 336 BC before this great enterprise could begin.

However, he was succeeded by his son Alexander III, 'the Great', who, after securing his control of Greece, took up his father's mantle and prepared his army for the invasion. In the spring of 334 BC Alexander's army of around

35,000 men crossed the Hellespont and landed in Asia Minor. At that time, the new Persian king Darius III was in his capital of Persepolis in modern-day Iran, and so left it to his local *satrap* (ruler) Arsites to deal with the Macedonian invasion. Having dealt with a Macedonian expedition two years before, Arsites was confident he could defeat Alexander.

One of Arsites' mercenary commanders, Memnon of Rhodes, recommended a 'scorched earth' policy – devastating the region to deny supplies to the enemy, while avoiding battle. Hunger would then deal with the Macedonian problem. Instead, though, Arsites decided to fight and in May, when Alexander reached the River Granicus (now the River Biga), he found the Persian army waiting for him beyond the far bank. He had around 18,000 men under his command – the rest of his army were too far behind him to intervene. Arsites commanded roughly twice as many men, including cavalry and a sizeable contingent of Greek mercenaries. After a brief council-of-war, Alexander decided to attack. He deployed his infantry in the centre, including his phalanx of Macedonian pikemen, and placed his cavalry on the wings. Alexander himself, accompanied by his elite lance-armed Companion cavalry, commanded the cavalry on the right wing.

Accounts of what followed vary, but it appears that the battle began with a cavalry attack across the river on the Macedonian right wing. Once the Persians on the far bank were fully engaged, Alexander unleashed the bulk of his Companions, followed by his infantry. In the general melee that followed, the Macedonians gradually overcame their opponents and began pushing them back. During the fight, Alexander supposedly killed Mithridates, Darius' son-in-law, with a lance thrust. The cavalry on the Persian left flank fled first, at which point the Persian infantry began to waver and run. Alexander decided not to pursue them, but instead reined in his men and launched them against the Greek mercenaries, who were quickly overwhelmed. The battle ended in a general rout, as the remaining Persians fled the field accompanied by Arsites. The Persian *satrap*, though, committed suicide before news of the defeat could reach the ears of King Darius. Of the 6,000 or so Persian casualties, at least half were Memnon's Greek mercenaries. Following the victory, Alexander established control over the Greek cities along the Aegean coast of Asia Minor, then marched east, deeper into the sprawling Persian Empire. Over the next ten years Alexander would conquer this empire and claim it for his own, before dying in Babylon in 323 BC, at the age of just 33.

LEFT When Alexander charged with his Companion cavalry he was conspicuous in his finery, which made him a target. Here, Alexander is shown surrounded by enemies before being rescued by 'Black Cleitus', the commander of his bodyguard, seen here fending off a blow from a Persian nobleman. (Richard Hook © Osprey Publishing)

CANNAE, 2 AUGUST 216 BC

A century after the campaigns of Alexander the Great, the new power in the Ancient World was the Roman Republic. After its foundation in the year 509 BC, the Republic witnessed the steady expansion of Roman power, expanding outwards from the city to encompass most of mainland Italy by 264 BC. During this expansion, Rome encountered and overcame a number of enemies, including the Gauls and Samnites, but when the Roman Senate continued its expansion beyond Italy, this brought the Republic into contact with new enemies. Chief amongst these was Carthage. The First Punic War (264–241 BC) was primarily fought in Sicily, the west of which was colonized by the North African state of Carthage. The Carthaginians were also a naval power, and in

order to defeat them the Romans had to build a fleet, which, after Sicily was conquered, they used to take the war to North Africa. This in turn led to Carthage suing for peace, and relinquishing control of Sicily, which became the first Roman colony.

The Carthaginians then expanded into Spain, but they felt they had a score to settle with Rome; another war was all but inevitable. It began in 218 BC as the gifted Carthaginian general Hannibal led an army from Spain into Gaul, and then across the Alps into Italy. The Roman armies sent to stop him were defeated at the battles of Trebbia (218 BC) and Lake Trasimene (217 BC). Hannibal then marched south, causing panic in Rome. In response the Roman Senate elected Quintus Fabius Maximus as 'dictator', a leader chosen in times of emergency to lead the defence of the Republic. His 'Fabian tactics' – the avoidance of battle – bought time for Rome to rebuild its military strength, but also left Hannibal free to ravage the countryside of southern Italy. Therefore, the dictatorship was revoked, and instead the consuls Lucius Aemilius Paulus and Gaius Terentius Varro were elected, with orders to defeat Hannibal.

A sizeable Roman and Latin allied army of more than 80,000 men was put into the field, and with Paulus and Varro at its head the Roman force confronted Hannibal near Cannae in Apulia. Hannibal's polyglot army of around 50,000 men included Gauls, Spaniards, Libyans and Numidians as well as Carthaginians. Hannibal anchored his left flank on a river and extended his line, to partly offset his lack of numbers. Then, as the Romans formed up and advanced towards him, the Carthaginian centre gave ground. As the lines eventually clashed, the two flanks of Hannibal's army enfolded the flanks of the Roman force. It was a classic pincer movement, and the Romans were soon trapped. Hemmed in on all sides, the Romans were cut down where they stood. As many as 50,000 Roman and Latin soldiers were killed in the battle, including Paulus, compared to around 8,000 of Hannibal's troops. Cannae marked the pinnacle of Hannibal's career. Ever since, Cannae has been seen as one of the classic battles of history, and one of the bloodiest. To the military scholar, Hannibal's great victory has come to be regarded as the timeless epitome of tactical perfection on the battlefield.

LEFT At Cannae, Hannibal gambled on the Romans concentrating their attack on his lightly held centre. Here, encouraged by Hannibal himself, his Gauls hold the Roman assault, their defence buying time for the rest of the army to envelop the Roman flanks. Hannibal's daring plan worked to perfection. (Peter Dennis © Osprey Publishing)

ZAMA, 19 OCTOBER 202 BC

After the Battle of Cannae, the Second Punic War between Rome and Carthage continued unabated for another 14 years. The Roman Republic raised more troops to make good their losses, and while several of their Italian allies switched their allegiance to Carthage, the Romans gradually won back control of most of southern Italy. The war then spread to Sicily and Spain, and while the Romans eventually secured control of Sicily, the campaign ebbed to and fro for 12 years before the Romans finally conquered the Iberian Peninsula. During this lengthy campaign Publius Cornelius Scipio 'Africanus' rose to prominence as a Roman leader whose abilities rivalled those of Hannibal himself. In 204 BC Scipio landed a Roman army in North

Africa, and the following year he soundly defeated a Carthaginian army at Utica. Scipio was now free to march on Carthage itself.

Before he did, though, Scipio needed to improve his strategic position, so he turned a key Carthaginian ally into a Roman one by encouraging the defection of Prince Masinissa of Numidia. As a result, when it invaded North Africa, Scipio's army was bolstered by large numbers of skilled Numidian cavalry. In Carthage, Hannibal and his remaining veterans were recalled from Italy to reinforce the battered Carthaginian army in North Africa. At stake in the battle ahead would be the very survival of Carthage. When last-minute peace talks failed, Scipio marched on Carthage, and Hannibal moved to intercept him. In mid-October 202 BC the two armies met at Zama in what is now Tunisia. Hannibal had around 40,000 men under his command, including 4,000 cavalry and 80 war elephants. Scipio's army was slightly smaller, but his legions were mostly veterans, and were supported by over 6,000 cavalry, many of them Numidians.

Hannibal began the battle by unleashing his elephants. Scipio's legions, though, sidestepped the charging animals, creating lanes through the Roman ranks, and the elephants were then surrounded and killed or else they stampeded. The two cavalry wings then met, the Romans helped by a number of stampeding elephants, which threw the Carthaginian horsemen into disarray. On both flanks the Roman cavalry routed their Carthaginian opponents and chased them from the field. This meant that the battle would now be decided by the main bodies of infantry. Scipio's legionaries advanced and the two sides clashed all along their front. With so much at stake the fighting was ferocious, but eventually the Carthaginians began to waver.

Hannibal had tried to thin out his line in an attempt to outflank the Roman infantry, just as he had done at Cannae. This time, however, Scipio matched the move and the battle continued. Then, when the victorious Roman cavalry returned from their pursuit, they fell upon the rear of the Carthaginian infantry. That was the crucial moment, and Hannibal's army began to disintegrate. Scipio's victory was complete. Although Hannibal escaped, most of his army was either killed or taken prisoner. The Roman casualties were around 2,500 men. With its last army destroyed, Carthage accepted crushing terms in exchange for a humiliating peace. The city would eventually be completely destroyed by the Romans in 146 BC. After Zama, Rome's mastery of the Mediterranean basin was assured.

LEFT The battle involved charges by elephants and cavalry melees, but the fight was decided by the main infantry clash. Here, Hastati from the Roman first line are pressed back by veteran Carthaginian Libyan-Phoenician spearmen, although the tide of battle eventually turned in Rome's favour. (Peter Dennis © Osprey Publishing)

CARRHAE, 53 BC

Following the final defeat of Carthage in 146 BC, the Roman Republic extended its influence around the Mediterranean basin. The richest of its new-won provinces lay in the east, including Syria, which was annexed by Pompey 'the Great' in 64 BC. Four years later Pompey became one of Rome's ruling triumvirate, together with Julius Caesar and Marcus Licinius Crassus, the richest man in Rome. As well as sharing power, each member of the triumvirate also exerted influence over part of Rome's territories. While Caesar campaigned in Gaul, and Pompey governed Spain and Rome, Crassus administered Syria. This brought him into contact with the neighbouring Parthian Empire. Although there was no pressing need, Crassus decided to invade

Parthia, largely to mirror the impressive martial achievements of Caesar and Pompey. This duly led to the greatest Roman military defeat since the Battle of Cannae.

The Parthian Empire was founded by Persian invaders in the 3rd century BC, and by 54 BC, when Crassus arrived in Syria, it covered most of modern-day Iraq and Iran. Its heartland, though, lay along the River Euphrates. The Parthians were a warlike people, ruled by a warrior caste, but they also adopted many of the cultural trappings of the earlier Persian Empire. However, in 57 BC the Empire had been riven by a war of succession between two royal brothers. When one of them, Orodes, emerged triumphant, his brother Mithridates fled to Syria and begged for help in reclaiming the throne. This was the *casus belli* Crassus needed. He raised an army of 30,000 legionaries supported by 4,000 cavalry led by his son Publius.

Ignoring advice to avoid the desert, Crassus marched directly across it. King Orodes II failed to anticipate this, and his main army was to the north. However, he sent a force of 10,000 men to delay any force attacking from the desert. This Parthian blocking force was led by the nobleman Surena, whose all-mounted force consisted of horse archers, supported by 1,000 heavily armoured cavalry, known as cataphracts. The two armies met near the town of Carrhae in Mesopotamia. Crassus formed his infantry into a square and continued his advance. Surena's horse archers harassed the Romans for several days, picking legionaries off as they advanced. The Parthian horsemen evaded all attempts by the legionaries to engage them.

When Publius Crassus launched his Gallic cavalry and some infantry supports out of the square to repel the Parthian light cavalry, they were lured into a trap sprung by the cataphracts. The Roman force was annihilated, and the younger Crassus was killed. His father's only hope now was that the horse archers would run out of arrows, but Surena had thought of that, and brought more supplies of them. At that point Crassus ordered his army to retreat to Carrhae, but order broke down, and most of the troops were isolated and cut down. Eventually, Crassus attempted to surrender, but was killed, at which point the remainder of his troops surrendered. It was a humiliating defeat for Rome, which lost its entire army. By contrast Parthian losses were light. The last casualty was Surena himself, who was executed after his victory by his jealous sovereign.

LEFT At Carrhae the Roman army led by Marcus Licinius Crassus had no means of countering the harrying archery of the Parthian light cavalry, and so was whittled down. After all attempts to drive the Parthians off failed, and following the death of Crassus, the Roman survivors were killed or captured. (Peter Dennis © Osprey Publishing)

ALESIA, 52 BC

In 60 BC, the establishment of the triumvirate between Julius Caesar, Pompey 'the Great' and Crassus guaranteed the political control of Rome by these three men. This brought a temporary abatement to the political turmoil that had plagued the Roman Republic. It also allowed the three men to divide control of Rome's provinces between them, and to further their own military careers. For his part, Caesar was appointed the governor of the Roman provinces of Gaul and Illyria. Caesar planned to use one of these, Transalpine Gaul (now southern France), as a springboard for a campaign to conquer all of Gaul. His *casus belli* was the invasion of non-Roman Gaul in 58 BC by the Gallic Helvetians, and then German tribes. A series of stunning

victories that year saw these invaders vanquished, but it also resulted in many Gallic tribes accepting Caesar's supremacy over them.

In 57–56 BC Caesar expanded his control of Gaul by campaigning against the northern Gallic tribes, until they too accepted Roman 'protection'. In 55 BC Caesar campaigned against the Germans to discourage further raids over the Rhine, and the following year he led the first of two annual expeditions to Britain, which secured the nominal submission of the southern British tribes. Back in Gaul, though, unrest against Roman rule had been growing. During the winter of 54–53 BC several northern tribes revolted, and Roman detachments were attacked. In the spring of 53 BC Caesar successfully campaigned against the Belgae, but the revolt then spread into central Gaul, where the tribes were united under the leadership of Vercingetorix. By the following spring, he had gathered an army of over 250,000 warriors.

In early 52 BC Caesar marched south, capturing several Gallic towns, but Vercingetorix skilfully avoided battle. Then, in July, Caesar finally caught up with the Gallic army near the headwaters of the River Seine. Vercingetorix and 80,000 of his men withdrew into the fortified hilltop stronghold of Alesia, and on reaching the place Caesar laid siege to it. In an unprecedented feat of military engineering the Romans then built over 14 miles of double wooden walls and ditches, which not only encircled Alesia, but protected the besiegers from an assault from the surrounding country. After all, Caesar knew that a Gallic army was massing to come to the aid of Vercingetorix. Meanwhile, inside Alesia, Vercingetorix attempted to send away his women and children to make his supplies last until help arrived. Caesar, though, refused to let them through his lines.

The Gallic relief force of some 240,000 men arrived in front of Caesar's siegeworks in mid-September. Although Caesar's 50,000 were hugely outnumbered, they successfully fought off three attempts to storm their defences. They also repulsed simultaneous sorties by Vercingetorix and his now-starving warriors. The double line of siegeworks held, and the now much reduced Gallic horde withdrew. It was now clear to Vercingetorix that his situation was hopeless. The day following the relieving army's withdrawal he led his men out of the fortress and surrendered to Caesar. He was eventually taken to Rome, and executed. For Caesar the rewards were huge. He successfully pacified the rest of Gaul, and the region would firmly remain part of Rome's dominions for another five centuries.

LEFT The most ferocious of the Gallic assaults on Caesar's defences was the last one, launched simultaneously from within and without the siege lines. For a time the Roman defenders were hard-pressed, but Caesar, pictured fighting bareheaded alongside his men, encouraged them to hold on. (Peter Dennis © Osprey Publishing)

PHARSALUS, 48 BC

Following the death of Crassus in 53 BC Rome was ruled jointly by Caesar and Pompey. But in 50 BC, Pompey seized control of Rome, and ordered Caesar to disband his army, or be branded an enemy of the Roman Republic. At the time Caesar was in Cisalpine Gaul – the Roman province of northern Italy – with just one legion. His response, in January 49 BC, was to cross the tiny River Rubicon, the symbolic boundary of Roman Italy, and march on Rome. Taken by surprise, Pompey and his supporters fled Rome and escaped to Greece, where they gathered their legions. Caesar responded by marching on Pompey's province of Spain, gathering his veteran Gallic legions along the way. By the end of 49 BC, Caesar had gained

control of the entire Western Mediterranean, and had been appointed 'dictator' by the Roman Senate. For his part Pompey consolidated his grip on Greece and the eastern provinces.

In early 48 BC, Caesar landed in Epirus in western Greece, and laid siege to Pompey's Adriatic base of Dyrrachium (now Dürres in Albania). Despite being outnumbered by Pompey, Caesar and his deputy Mark Antony used the same engineering skills they had displayed at Alesia to encircle the port, but in early July Pompey counter-attacked, forcing Caesar to withdraw. Caesar regrouped in nearby Thessaly, and Pompey hurried to bring him to battle. The two sides met near Pharsalus in central Greece. Pompey had around 60,000 legionaries under his command, and 7,000 cavalry, while Caesar could muster just 30,000 legionaries, and 1,000 horsemen. The bulk of Caesar's army, though, were battle-hardened veterans of the Gallic wars.

The two armies deployed in the usual way, with one flank anchored on the small River Enipeas. This allowed both sides to deploy their cavalry on their exposed flank. The Caesarian army was more thinly spread than Pompey's, but Caesar kept back a small reserve which he used to support his outnumbered horsemen. Then Caesar began the battle, advancing his legionaries towards the enemy lines. When they clashed, Pompey unleashed his cavalry, which forced back their Caesarian rivals. At that critical moment, Caesar personally led his reserve, taking Pompey's horsemen and supporting light infantry by surprise. They scattered, which allowed Caesar to swing his reserve inwards against the exposed left flank of Pompey's legions.

Caesar then re-joined his main body of infantry, leading his rearmost lines forward to relieve the men in the front of the fight. His veterans did Caesar proud, their ranks parting to let the fresh legionaries through. This, together with the flank attack, proved too much for Pompey's less experienced legions, who began to waver. Soon the Pompeian army broke completely, and fled back to their camp. Caesar's men duly stormed it, routing Pompey's own veteran legionaries, then pursuing the enemy army. Pompey escaped, but over 6,000 of his men were killed in the battle, and many more captured. Caesar's losses amounted to 1,500 men. Later, Caesar pursued Pompey to Egypt, only to discover his great rival had been murdered. After Pharsalus, Julius Caesar became the master of the Roman world.

LEFT At Pharsalus, Pompey had considerably more cavalry, so Caesar supported his own horse with legionaries. This proved highly effective, as Caesar used his infantry to counter-attack when the impetus of the Pompeian cavalry was spent, and routed the enemy horsemen. (Adam Hook © Osprey Publishing)

ACTIUM, 31 BC

In 44 BC, Julius Caesar was murdered by those who opposed his dictatorship. The assassins fled to Greece to raise an army, and were pursued there by Caesar's former deputies Mark Antony and Marcus Lepidus, and Caesar's adopted nephew Octavian. The three formed a triumvirate and swore to avenge Caesar. In 42 BC the Republicans were defeated at the Battle of Philippi, and the leading assassins Brutus and Cassius were killed. The Roman provinces were divided among the victors, with Octavian and Lepidus ruling the west and Antony the east. Lepidus was eventually dropped from the triumvirate. Then, in 33 BC, the two remaining rulers fell out. While in Egypt, Antony had become besotted with Cleopatra, and so he

divorced his wife Octavia – Octavian's sister – and married the Egyptian queen instead.

An incensed Octavian forced the Roman Senate to declare war on Antony and Cleopatra. By then, Antony had moved to Greece, where he gathered an army to defend his eastern provinces. Any plans to invade Italy were thwarted by Octavian's sizeable fleet, commanded by Marcus Agrippa. In 31 BC Octavian landed in Epirus at the head of an equally powerful army. By then Antony had a fleet of his own, supplied by Cleopatra, which he stationed in the Ambracian Gulf, which emptied into the Aegean. Octavian marched his army south, and by late August the two rival armies were encamped on either side of the gulf. Agrippa's fleet had also arrived, and blockaded the entrance to the gulf thereby trapping the Antonine fleet.

Antony and Cleopatra decided that their best chance lay in a sea battle. If they lost they expected to be able to escape to Egypt to raise more forces, leaving their army to march home overland. Soon after dawn on 2 September the Antonine fleet put to sea, passing through the mouth of the gulf into the open sea. The Octavian fleet was formed into three squadrons, with Agrippa leading the left-hand one. In theory he had around 400 galleys – considerably more than Antony, who commanded around 250 larger warships, plus around 50 transport ships filled with troops. In fact both fleets were probably much smaller, probably around half these totals, as the Octavian fleet still hadn't concentrated off the gulf, and Antony's fleet was undermanned due to desertion. Antony's fleet was divided into four squadrons, including a reserve led by Cleopatra herself.

As both commanders hoped to overpower the enemy's northern wing, the fighting was fiercest there. This sea battle was decided by ramming, and by the torsion-powered artillery mounted in the larger vessels. The outcome, though, remained in the balance throughout the afternoon. Then, Cleopatra's reserve squadron moved forward, heading around the southern end of the melee. Rather than turn to fall on Agrippa's fleet, though, it continued on towards the south, and disappeared. She had abandoned Antony, who set off in pursuit with his own squadron. Agrippa was then able to overpower the remains of the demoralized Antonine fleet, although many of the ships had been set alight by their crews before being abandoned. The Octavian victory marked the end of Antony's rule, and the following year, as Octavian closed in on Alexandria, both he and Cleopatra committed suicide. Octavian, soon to be the Emperor Augustus, was now the unchallenged ruler of the dying Roman Republic.

LEFT The climax of the battle came in mid-afternoon. Although outnumbered, Antony's fleet had held its own. Cleopatra's reserve squadron could still make a difference. However, after it fled the battle, taking the queen with it, Antony's remaining ships were overwhelmed. (Christa Hook © Osprey Publishing)

THE TEUTOBURGERWALD, AD 9

After securing control of the Roman world, the Emperor Augustus set about strengthening its borders. A series of frontier defences were created, and buffer states created to safeguard the 'Pax Romana'. The most volatile stretch of frontier lay north of the Alps, along the River Rhine, which divided Roman Gaul to the west from the fierce German tribes to their west.

Following Germanic raids into Gaul early in his reign, Augustus favoured an expansion of this frontier eastwards, to create more of a buffer zone. Ideally, he favoured pushing Rome's frontier as far as the River Elbe. Augustus' adopted sons Tiberius and Drusus both campaigned there, and by AD 4 the German lands between the rivers Rhine and Weser had

become loyal to Rome. A revolt in the Roman Balkan provinces of Illyria and Pannonia, though, meant that Tiberius left to restore order there, and left the German frontier in the hands of his less experienced deputy, Publius Quinctilius Varus.

Varus had several legions under his command, augmented by numerous auxiliary troops, many of whom were German. His orders were to safeguard the border area of Germania, while extending Roman reach beyond the River Weser. In AD 9 he embarked on a summer campaign east of the river with three legions. One of his auxiliary commanders was a German known as Arminius, a prince of the pro-Roman Cheruscii tribe. He, though, had secretly been planning a revolt, and by that summer had built up an alliance of German tribes. That autumn, towards the end of the season's campaign, Varus learned that a nearby tribe had revolted against Roman rule. He decided to lead a punitive raid on the tribe, unaware that the report had been fabricated by Arminius. As Varus marched north, his army came within reach of the large army of German tribes which Arminius had brought together. All Arminius had to do was to spring his trap.

This took place in the Teutoburgerwald, a large, wooded area in what is now the Osnabruck region of Lower Saxony. Here, Varus' route was constricted by a high hill on one side and a marsh on the other. Arminius had an unknown number of German tribesmen at his command – probably around 20,000 men – while Varus commanded around 16,000, most of whom were Roman legionaries. In open terrain the Roman drill and training would have guaranteed victory. In these woods, though, with the Roman column strung out over several miles, the terrain favoured the Germans. In what became a running battle Arminius managed to overwhelm parts of the Roman column, forcing the rest into a 'killing ground' where an earthen wall blocked the obvious escape route from the forest.

Faced with certain defeat, Varus committed suicide, leaving his legionaries to escape as best they could. Only a few made it – virtually the entire Roman force was killed or captured, while German losses were relatively minor. Following the disaster, the Romans returned to their Rhine frontier, and while punitive expeditions into Germany continued, all plans to expand the Empire to the Elbe were abandoned.

LEFT For three days, Publius Quinctilius Varus' Roman army was harassed by German attacks, and lost its cohesion as it marched through the Teutoburgerwald. There, Arminius was able to ambush these isolated detachments, and so destroy almost all of the Roman force. (Peter Dennis © Osprey Publishing)

STRASBOURG, AD 357

For over three centuries the Roman Empire remained largely untroubled by large-scale invasion. Instead, the Roman world was riven by intermittent struggles for power by rival claimants to the Imperial throne. For the most part, Rome's wars involved operations on the frontier, in northern Britain, along the Rhine and Danube, and in the east, against the Parthians and their Sassanid successors. The German frontier remained troublesome, particularly when internal wars frequently stripped it of some of its best troops. In AD 350 it was divided into eastern and western portions, ruled by the Emperors Constans and Constantius II, both sons of Constantine 'the Great'. However, when Constans was murdered by

Magnentius, one of his generals, his brother headed west to seek revenge.

The armies of Magnentius and Constantius converged on the Balkans, where they fought each other to a standstill in a civil war that cost Rome the best of its legions. On the Rhine frontier the Alemanni – a confederation of German tribes – overran the denuded forts there, and together with the Franks they crossed the river to raid deep into Roman Gaul. After Magnentius died in AD 353 Constantius did what he could to restore order, but he now lacked the troops to drive out the invaders, and to protect the rest of his empire as well. Therefore, in AD 355 he appointed his cousin Julian as 'Caesar' (vice emperor) to regain control of Gaul, while he returned to the east. Throughout AD 356 Julian campaigned in central Gaul, then marched to the Rhine frontier, to recapture Colonia Agrippina (Cologne). Julian now lay between the Alemanni and their Germanic homeland.

In response, 35,000 Alemanni warriors gathered near Argentoratum (Strasbourg), under the command of the high-king Chnodomar. Confidently, Julian marched to meet him with 15,000 men, and in mid-August he came upon the Alemanni arrayed on a ridge to the south of the city. The two battle lines advanced towards each other and clashed, the Germans supported by archers firing from the cover of a nearby forest. On the Roman right Julian's cavalry charged, but were broken by the Alemanni horsemen who were led by Chnodomar himself. He then turned to attack the Roman right flank, which began to give way. In the centre the tribesman reached the Roman second line, but it held its ground. On the Roman left the Germans were pushed back. Meanwhile Julian rallied the Roman right, which also began to gain ground. Eventually the Alemanni wavered and broke, and fled towards the safety of the Rhine. Chnodomar, though, was captured by the pursuing Romans.

The battle had saved Gaul, and cost the lives of more than 8,000 barbarians. Afterwards, Julian finished restoring the Rhine frontier, and in AD 360 he was proclaimed emperor by his men. He acceded to the purple fully the next year, following the death of Constantius. Julian, nicknamed 'the Apostate' by Christians, would subsequently campaign against the Sassanids, until his death in Mesopotamia in AD 363.

LEFT A ferocious charge by Chnodomar's German warriors broke through the centre of the Roman line, but elsewhere the shield wall held firm. Eventually, the Roman commander Julian was able to rally his centre, and his legionaries were then able to repulse the assault. (Florent Vincent © Osprey Publishing)

ADRIANOPLE, AD 378

Around the middle of the 4th century AD the nomadic and warlike Huns appeared on the eastern fringe of modern-day Europe. They had migrated eastwards from the steppes of Central Asia, and as they went they fought and then displaced the peoples they encountered. Their first victims were the Alans, who fled westwards, which in turn displaced the Gothic kingdoms in what is now Ukraine and Romania. By AD 376, huge numbers of Goth refugees had reached the frontier of the Eastern Roman Empire, which ran along the River Danube. They petitioned to be allowed to settle in the Empire, but bureaucracy and distance made these negotiations a lengthy process. Eventually they were allowed to cross the Danube, but they soon

found themselves persecuted by the local Roman administrators and army, who saw them as a source of *foederati* (auxiliary warriors) and slaves. Complaints were met with punitive military action, which led in turn to a full-scale revolt by the Goths against their Roman overlords.

The Eastern Roman Emperor Valens and his army were busy campaigning in Syria, so he begged his nephew, the Western Emperor Gratian, for troops, who contained the Goths in Thrace. Then, in June AD 378, Valens and his main army reached Constantinople, which he used for his campaign against the Goths. He estimated the Goth army, led by Fritigern, had around 10,000 men under arms. By then Gratian's troops were further east, dealing with more Germanic incursions into the province of Pannonia, further up the Danube. However, Valens' deputy Sebastianus had remained in Thrace and had succeeded in containing Fritigern's army around the city of Adrianople in eastern Thrace, so Valens advanced into Thrace and in late June he reached the city. Peace negotiations failed; therefore, on 9 August he marched out of Adrianople to engage Fritigern, whose army was encamped nearby. The exact location of the battlefield is now unknown.

Valens had around 15,000 troops under his command, a third of whom were cavalry. The core of his infantry was made up of three Roman legions. Fritigern's army was also a mixed force of foot and horse, and was roughly the same size as its opponent's force. The Goths had deployed on top of a hill, dominated by a laager of wagons which protected the non-combatants. Grass was burned so the smoke would screen their deployment from the Romans, but essentially Fritigern grouped his infantry in front of the wagons, while his cavalry were hidden by the smoke on either flank. More negotiations followed, but some of the impatient Roman infantry began skirmishing with the Goths, and this brought on a full-scale battle.

The Roman legions began advancing towards the wagon laager, and while Valens' right wing was held, his left pushed the Goth infantry back as far as the wagons. At that moment, though, the Goth cavalry fell on the Roman flanks, and Valens' army was encircled. The disordered Romans broke, and were hacked down as they fled. Only a third of Valens' army escaped the debacle, and the emperor himself was killed during the rout. This disaster stripped the Eastern Roman Empire of some of its best troops, but the real loss was to prestige. The centuries-old aura of Roman invincibility had been stripped away, and the Roman frontier had been breached. Just 40 years later, the Goths would sack Rome itself.

LEFT At Adrianople the Goths, led by their warlord Fritigern, were able to drive off the Roman cavalry on the flanks, and then envelop the Roman centre. Surrounded, the outnumbered veteran legionaries fought on, protecting Emperor Valens until they were all cut down. (Howard Gerrard © Osprey Publishing)

CHÂLONS (OR THE CATALAUNIAN FIELDS), AD 451

Around AD 370, the westward migration of the nomadic Huns reached the Volga basin and displaced the Goths, who moved towards the Danubian frontier of the Roman Empire. This, though, was only the first of these displacements. Over the next half century, the warlike Huns continued their slow drift westwards, displacing other peoples who lay in their path. These included the Gepids, the Sarmatians, the Alemanni and the Lombards. From AD 434 on, they were commanded by Atilla, who led devastating major raids across the Danube into

the Eastern Roman Empire. His Hun horsemen even reached the walls of Constantinople itself. Until AD 450 he left the Western Roman Empire alone. After all, it was an empire in name alone – by the mid-5th century AD it had become a confederation of Romans, Visigoths and others, and was no longer the bastion of civilization and order it had once been.

Then, in AD 449, Atilla was offered half of the Western Empire, if he invaded it and dealt with the Visigoths who occupied most of Gaul. He duly made peace with the Eastern Empire, and in early AD 451 he crossed the Rhine frontier into Gaul. Advancing down the Moselle, Atilla's vast army overwhelmed and sacked Trier, Metz and Reims, and then bypassed Paris to lay siege to Aurelianum (Orléans). Most of these former Roman cities were now ruled by Rome's Frankish and Alan allies. This invasion incensed the Western Emperor Valentian III, who sent his best general Flavius Aetius to try and deal with the situation.

Aetius gathered a coalition army of Romans, Franks, Alans and Visigoths – around 40,000–60,000 men – and in May he marched north to relieve Aurelianum. Although Atilla commanded a similarly sized army, when word of this new threat reached him he broke off the half-hearted

siege and withdrew to the east. However, Aetius caught up with the Hun horde and on 20 June he brought it to battle at the Catalaunian Fields near Châlons. This was a flat plain, dominated by a slope which ended in a ridge. Aetius deployed his Romans in the centre, with the Visigoths on his right and his other Germanic allies on his left. All three wings of his army contained a mix of infantry and cavalry. The Huns, though, were primarily a mounted force, and Atilla deployed his heavier cavalry in the centre, and his numerous light horse archers on its flanks.

The battle began in the late afternoon as Aetius' army advanced towards the ridge. They occupied part of it, and the Huns the other part, and the battle soon became a struggle for control of this high ground. In the swirling melee that followed, King Theodoric of the Visigoths was killed, but the Huns were driven back to the shelter of their camp – a huge wagon laager. The exhausted combatants broke off the fight at sunset, and during the night Atilla decided to withdraw. His battered horde withdrew to the Rhine, and continued eastwards into what is now Hungary. The Western Roman Empire had been spared, thanks to a skilled Roman general, and a loose confederation of barbarian tribes, fighting to preserve their new homeland.

LEFT The Romans, led by Flavius Aetius, were hard-pressed by the Hun mounted archers, but unlike their Visigoth allies the Roman infantry held their ground. Their shield wall also held in the face of repeated assaults by Germanic cavalry, and so helped turn the tide of battle. (Peter Dennis © Osprey Publishing)

THE MEDIEVAL WORLD

CONSTANTINOPLE, AD 718

In AD 620, encouraged by the Prophet Mohammed, the historical phenomenon known as the Arab Conquests began. This rapid expansion of the Islamic sphere of influence from Arabia began with the dismemberment of Sassanid Persia, then the conquest of the Byzantine provinces of Syria and Egypt. This was achieved by military conquest, but was followed by the foundation and spread of Islamic belief, and its attendant systems of law and government. By the mid-7th century AD this Islamic influence had spread at sword point along the coast of North Africa, and eastwards into Persia and Afghanistan. In the AD 630s the Byzantine Empire, the successor of the Eastern Roman Empire, attempted to stem the Islamic tide in

eastern Asia Minor by military means. However, in the 'Battle of the Masts' in AD 655, an Arab fleet wrested naval control of the Eastern Mediterranean from the Byzantines.

In AD 674 the Arabs besieged the Byzantine capital of Constantinople for the first time. The siege was broken by the Byzantine army, but it was now clear that the Byzantine Empire was fighting for its very survival. Then, in AD 715, Sulayman, the Arab Caliph of Syria's ruling Umayyad Dynasty, decided to renew the Arab assault on the Byzantine Empire. He ordered his nephew Maslama ibn Abd al Malik to lead a major offensive, with the ultimate objective of capturing the Byzantine capital. It was hoped that the Byzantines would be too distracted by dynastic strife resulting from rival familial claims to the throne to repel the offensive. Maslama, a gifted commander, invaded Asia Minor the following year, and by the spring of AD 717 he crossed the Dardanelles, aided by the Arab fleet which had joined him from Syria. A powerful Arab army now stood on the shores of Europe.

Maslama advanced on Constantinople, and by August he had invested the city on its landward side. The arrival of the Arab fleet completed the investment of the city. The Arab naval commander had hoped to breach the city's defences from seaward, but one of his squadrons was destroyed by a defending Byzantine squadron, and the attempt was called off. The Byzantine success was due to the use of 'Greek Fire' – a flamethrower system which projected flaming naphtha onto the enemy ships. Fearing further attacks, the fleet withdrew further up the Bosphorus. This allowed the Byzantine emperor Leo III to send supply ships across the Bosphorus to resupply the city. By contrast, during the winter the Arab army began to run short of provisions, having already stripped the Thracian countryside for food.

In September 1717 Sulayman died of natural causes, and was succeeded by his cousin Umar ibn Abd al-Aziz, who became the Caliph Umar II. In late AD 717 Umar sent warships and supplies from Egypt and North Africa to bolster the siege. However, Leo ordered his fleet to attack this new fleet as it lay at anchor on the Asian shore of the Bosphorus. Again, Greek Fire proved the key to victory for the Byzantines, and these new ships and the vital supplies they carried were destroyed. The Arab army now came under attack by a Bulgar army, which had intervened in the struggle in support of the Byzantines. The Arab besiegers immediately found themselves between two armies. Finally, in August of AD 718, Umar II ordered Maslama to lift the siege and withdraw to the ships. The siege of Constantinople had been lifted, and the Byzantine Empire had survived. As a result, it remained a key bulwark against Islamic expansion for another seven centuries.

LEFT The decisive moment in the siege of Constantinople came in September when the small war galleys ('dromons') of the Byzantine navy fell upon an isolated squadron of the Umayyad fleet in the Bosphorus. There, they used the fearsome new technology of Greek Fire and systematically destroyed their opponents. (Graham Turner © Osprey Publishing)

TOURS, 25 OCTOBER AD 732

In AD 711, the Arab conquest reached the shores of Spain near Gibraltar when a raiding army crossed over from North Africa. The following year they defeated a Christian Visigothic army, and by the end of the decade over two-thirds of the Iberian Peninsula lay in Arab hands. The Arab Umayyad Dynasty who spearheaded this invasion called their new province Al-Andalus.

The Umayyad Caliphate now stretched from the Atlantic Ocean to the borders of India. Effectively, Christian territory in Iberia was now limited to the southern foothills of the Pyrenees.

By AD 720, Arab armies had crossed the mountains to campaign in the Frankish realm – formerly Roman Gaul. The following year, this campaign of conquest was halted at Toulouse,

when the Umayyad governor of Al-Andalus was defeated by a Christian Frankish army led by the Duke Odo 'the Great' of Aquitaine. This Arab defeat prevented any further large-scale incursions across the Pyrenees for a decade. However, in AD 732 a new Umayyad governor, Abd al-Rahman al-Ghafiqui, renewed the offensive and defeated Duke Odo at the Battle of the River Garonne, fought near Bordeaux. The city was also captured by the Arabs. Duke Odo escaped with the remnants of his army, and sent pleas for help to Charles Martel, the 'mayor' (de facto leader) of the Merovingian Franks. In return for Odo's fealty to Charles, and the integration of his duchy into the Frankish realm, Charles Martel agreed to march south and face the Arab army in battle.

After defeating Odo, Abd al-Rahman launched raids into the Merovingian kingdom, but on hearing that a Merovingian army was mustering at Tours on the River Loire he marched northwards, towards the River Loire, his army plundering what it could along the way. He had around 15,000–20,000 battle-seasoned Arab warriors at his back, and was confident he could overpower any force the Merovingians sent to fight him. The sources are vague about the details of what happened next, but they agree on the main points. In mid-October the vanguards of both armies clashed south of Tours, near the River Vienne. Abd al-Rahman set up his camp south of the river and prepared his army for battle. Charles, though, was eager for a fight too. He crossed the river, then drew up his army of around 12,000 men near the Arab camp, on ground of his own choosing. As a result, Abd al-Rahman had little option but to attack him.

The Arab army was predominantly a cavalry force, and Abd al-Rahman led his horsemen in a thunderous assault against the Frankish infantry. To his surprise the assault was repulsed. He pulled back to his camp, at which point Duke Odo, having outflanked the Arab army, fell on the camp with his own cavalry. In the ensuing melee Abd al-Rahman was killed, and while the Frankish horse were repulsed, it was clear that the leaderless army had to retreat. The Arabs withdrew under cover of darkness, and returned to Al-Andalus. The battle was a pivotal moment in European history. The Islamic tide had been stemmed, and the Frankish realm had been strengthened. It would soon develop into a powerful kingdom, which in turn would evolve into France. The victory at Tours, though, guaranteed it would no longer be threatened by Arab invasion.

LEFT After repulsing a charge by the Umayyad cavalry led by Abd al-Rahman, the Frankish leader Charles Martel pursued the enemy back to their camp. Although the Frankish assault that followed was driven off, Abd al-Rahman was killed, and his now leaderless army withdrew. (Graham Turner © Osprey Publishing)

HASTINGS, 10 OCTOBER 1066

Arguably the most famous battle fought on British soil, Hastings decided the fate of a kingdom. Essentially, it was the climax of a fight for succession which began in January 1066 with the death of the Anglo-Saxon English king Edward the Confessor. The English Harold Godwinson was named as his successor, but the crown was also claimed by his brother Tostig, Duke William of Normandy, and the Norwegian king Harald III 'Hardrada'. As Harold was being crowned, the rivals to the throne began to lay plans to invade England and seize the crown for themselves. The first assault came from Tostig, who raided the coast of northern England before being driven off. He then allied himself with King Harald, and together they landed in northern England that September.

Harald defeated the local English army at Fulford, while King Harold was on England's south coast, waiting for an invasion from Normandy. Harold forced-marched his army northwards, and on 20 September met Harald and Tostig at Stamford Bridge to the east of York. It was a hard-fought battle, but eventually the Anglo-Saxons emerged victorious, and both Harald and Tostig were killed. Eight days later, Duke William landed near Pevensey on the south coast of England. Therefore, Harold's battered army had to force-march south again, to deal with this new threat.

That summer, Duke William had assembled a 700-ship invasion fleet and used it to transport an army of around 6,500 men across the Channel. Its core consisted of 2,000 mounted Norman knights, armed with lances, but the army also contained sizeable contingents of spearmen and archers. The crossing was delayed by bad weather, but William eventually disembarked on English soil on 28 September. He consolidated his beachhead around Pevensey and Hastings, and prepared to march on London. King Harold, though, appeared to the north of Hastings on 13 October, and took up position on Senlac Hill. He had around 7,000 infantry under his command, including up to 2,000 veteran 'huscarls' armed primarily with two-handed axes, who made up the king's personal guard. The following morning, Duke William advanced to give battle.

Harold was in a strong position, his shield wall arrayed at the top of the gently sloping hill, with his flanks protected by marshland. Thus, William had no option but to launch a frontal attack. Still, he used his thousand archers to weaken the English line, supported by his cavalry. Duke William then sent in his spearmen, hoping to exploit any gaps the arrows had caused in the English line. However, Harold's men stood their ground, and the battle ground on. This was very much a battle of attrition, and for most of the day every Norman assault was repulsed. At one stage, when the Norman left wing was thrown back, it was thought William had been killed, so the Duke took off his helmet, and rallied his wavering troops by showing he was still in command of them.

Then, thinking the Normans were fleeing, parts of the English army began to advance in pursuit. Grasping his chance, William led his cavalry in a counter-attack, and routed the pursuers. He then launched an all-out attack on the weakened English line, and this time it broke. In the slaughter that followed, King Harold was killed, together with 4,000 of his men, including most of his elite huscarls. William's losses were roughly half that number. Effectively, Anglo-Saxon England died that day. After his victory, William completed his conquest of Harold's kingdom, and on Christmas Day he was crowned King of England.

LEFT At the height of the battle the rumour spread that Duke William had been killed. He then rode among the Norman ranks with his helmet raised, to prove to his men he was still alive. Here, he exhorts his men to rally and attack again, encouraged by his brother, Bishop Odo. (Angus McBride © Osprey Publishing)

MANZIKERT, 26 AUGUST 1071

The Byzantine Empire weathered the storm of the Arab Conquests of the 7th and early 8th centuries AD, and largely due to its highly organized military infrastructure it kept the Muslim armies at bay. In the mid-11th century, though, poor imperial leadership led to the neglect of the Byzantine military machine. Unfortunately for the empire, this coincided with the appearance of the Seljuk Turks, a warlike Muslim people from Central Asia who seized control of the Arab lands of Persia, Mesopotamia and parts of Syria as well as Anatolia. This brought them into direct contact with the eastern portion of the Byzantine Empire. After some initial campaigning, the Byzantines signed a peace treaty with the Seljuks,

who at first were more interested in attacking the Fatimid Caliphate in Egypt.

From 1067 on, the new Byzantine emperor Romanus Diogenes busied himself rebuilding his army and his empire's eastern defences. However, in 1070, when the emperor was away campaigning in Italy, the Turks led by Arp Arslan invaded the Byzantine Empire again, defeating a Byzantine army at Sebasteia in eastern Asia Minor and capturing the Byzantine stronghold of Manzikert in Byzantine Armenia. Romanus Diogenes hastened to Constantinople, and in early 1071 he led his army east through Asia Minor. His objective was the recapture of Manzikert. His army of around 25,000 men included veteran Byzantine regulars, as well as less reliable mercenaries. To counter it, Alp Arslan advanced from Syria with a similarly sized army, much of which was cavalry.

On reaching Armenia, Romanus sent a strong detachment to secure the town of Ahlat, while the rest of his army advanced on Manzikert. Arp Aslan responded by falling on the isolated detachment at Ahlat and defeating it. He then marched to confront the Byzantine army at Manzikert. Romanus rejected all peace offers, and instead he elected to give battle. He organised his army into four divisions, one of which formed a reserve. By contrast Arp Arslan deployed in a crescent shape, with a centre and two wings of cavalry.

Romanus' central division of heavy Varangian infantry and armoured cavalry advanced on the Turks, forcing them back. Then the rest of the Byzantine army advanced in support. The dust thrown up by this hid the Turkish crescents, though, which enclosed the Byzantine flanks as they advanced. The Seljuk light cavalry then harried the Byzantines, who were unwilling to pursue them into the dust cloud. Gradually the Byzantine army became disordered and its flanks were driven back.

At that point Alp Arslan ordered a general advance and soon the centre of the Byzantine army was surrounded. In the fighting that followed, Romanus was captured, but most of his best troops were killed. The rest of his army fled the field. Over 6,000 Byzantines were killed or captured at Manzikert, while Turkish losses were minimal. This was less important, though, than the strategic consequences of the battle. The Byzantine Empire had been humiliated, and would soon be plunged into civil war. It would shortly face a fight for survival against an ascendant Seljuk Empire.

LEFT At the close of the battle, as the wings of his army fled the field, the Byzantine emperor Romanus and his bodyguard were cut off by the Turks and forced to make a last stand. They were cut down, and the emperor, pictured here sword in hand, was eventually captured. (Christa Hook © Osprey Publishing)

HATTIN, 4 JULY 1187

In 1097, Pope Urban II called on Western Europe to launch a Holy Crusade to liberate Jerusalem from 'the infidel'. It was a plea that appealed to Christendom's power-hungry feudal nobility, and soon Crusading armies were on the march. It would be two centuries before this Crusading zeal finally burned itself out. During the First Crusade (1096–99), a Crusading army was unleashed on the Islamic states of the Middle East and, despite causing friction with the Byzantines, they succeeded on reaching Jerusalem. They were helped by a lack of unity among the Muslim States following rivalry between the Seljuk Empire and the Fatimid Caliphate. The Seljuks were also riven by internal strife, which continued until the mid-12th century. Following the capture of

Jerusalem many of the Crusaders returned home to Europe, but a handful remained to govern their newly created Crusader States in the Levant, under the titular leadership of King Baldwin, King of Jerusalem. Islamic pressure on these states led to the Second Crusade (1147–49), another military intervention led by the King of France and the German emperor. Disagreement between the leaders, however, led the crusade to founder in 1148 during a campaign to capture Damascus.

Military pressure on the Crusader States continued during the later 12th century when the focus of conflict shifted from Syria to Egypt. The weak Fatimid Caliphate seemed ripe for attack, and both the Crusaders and the Seljuks coveted the richest land in the Middle East. Ultimately, though, neither Crusader nor Turk gained control. Instead, the new Ayyubid dynasty rose to prominence, displacing the Fatimids. In 1169 the Kurdish commander Salah ed-Din (or Saladin) became the Egyptian *wazire* – the de facto master of Egypt. During the next decade his well-trained Mamluk army gained control of Syria, uniting the Levant into one political entity. By 1183 Saladin had effectively encircled the Crusader States. Four years later, he made his move.

In June 1187, after declaring a Jihad ('Holy War'), Saladin invaded the Crusader States, laying siege to Tiberias on the Sea of Galilee. The new Crusading ruler, King Guy of Jerusalem, gathered an army at Acre and marched east in an attempt to raise the siege. Instead, when he was still ten miles to the west of the besieged town, he encountered a large force of Muslim skirmishers. These harassed the Christian column as they crossed the Plain of Toran, and so Guy ordered a fortified camp to be set up. The skirmishers, though, prevented them from reaching the nearest source of water, the springs below the distinctive rock outcrop known as the Horns of Hattin.

At dawn on 4 July the Crusaders formed up into battle array, but Saladin laid a smoke screen of burning grass, which completely disoriented the Crusaders. The Crusaders were harried by mounted archers, and their losses mounted steadily. Then, using the smoke as cover, Saladin's cavalry isolated the enemy's rearguard, and cut it to pieces. The fight then turned into a running battle, as groups of Crusaders tried to escape, or to find water. Guy tried to make a last stand, but in the end lack of water forced them to surrender. By day's end, most of the Crusading army of 20,000 men had been killed or captured. Muslim losses were minimal. Saladin's great victory meant that the Crusader States now lay at his mercy. Over the next two years he would overrun most of them and recapture Jerusalem before his death in 1193. However, other crusades would follow, and the fight for 'The Holy Land' would continue for another century.

LEFT The thirsty demoralized Crusader army was brought to battle beneath the Horns of Hattin, but they still repulsed several Saracen attacks before being overwhelmed. Here, the great Saracen leader Saladin watches the final assault, accompanied by his excited son af-'Afdal. (Peter Dennis © Osprey Publishing)

LAKE PEIPUS, 5 APRIL 1242

During the High Middle Ages, war fought on religious grounds was not limited to the Crusading States of the Levant. As the Crusading movement lost ground in the Middle East, it increasingly became an impetus for conflict in Eastern Europe. The Germanic states of Central Europe viewed the Estonian and Russian peoples to the east as 'barbarians', and a threat to the Christian states of Finland, Sweden and Livonia. The real problem, however, was the rising power of the Republic of Novgorod. This was a Russian city state that embraced the Byzantine Orthodox church rather than the Romanized Latin one. In the eyes of the Latin church this made them 'pagan', and therefore a suitable target for Northern Crusaders.

During the early 12th century the city had come to dominate the fur trade in the Baltic, and strong trading links had developed between Novgorod and the Scandinavian kingdoms. Growing religious intolerance, though, led to trade embargos, and to Crusading expeditions launched from the Baltic States and Sweden. In 1240 the Swedes had attempted to seize control of the mouth of the River Neva, where the city of St. Petersburg now stands. This invasion had been repulsed thanks to the intervention of the teenage Prince Alexander of Novgorod. However, another threat then developed to the west. That spring a Crusading army spearheaded by the Livonian Teutonic Knights, a military order, invaded the rich city state of Pskov, and by autumn the city had been captured and a puppet ruler installed. Pskov was an ally of Novgorod; therefore, the Republic became embroiled in this new war.

After the battle against the Swedes, Prince Alexander had been given the cognomen 'Nevsky' (of the Neva), and that winter he was recalled to Novgorod. In the summer of 1241, he managed to recapture Pskov while the Crusaders were campaigning in Estonia. The fighting resumed in the spring of 1242, before the snows melted. The Teutonic Order led by Deitrich von Grüningen joined forces with Prince-Bishop Hermann of Dorpat and his auxiliaries to drive out the Russian troops who were stationed in the bishopric. The combined army then headed east to Lake Peipus, the border with Novgorod.

The lake was still frozen over; therefore, it presented an ideal invasion route. Alexander Nevsky's army, though, were waiting for them on the western side of the narrowest part of the frozen lake. The armies were of roughly the same size, and consisted mainly of lightly armed troops, apart from the 500 or so Crusading knights – the core of the army. The battle began soon after daybreak on 5 April, as after forming a wedge the knights charged across the ice to attack Nevsky's spearmen. The knights smashed through the Russian ranks, but Nevsky counter-attacked with his own lighter cavalry, and the now disorganized knights broke. The Novgorod cavalry pursued them, and according to the chronicles many of the knights drowned as the ice broke under their weight. Novgorod was saved but soon a new threat – the Mongols – would fall upon the Republic from the east. The 'battle on the ice' was later immortalized in Sergei Eisenstein's classic silent film *Alexander Nevsky* (1938).

LEFT The deciding moment came when Alexander unleashed his light cavalry, who fell upon the wings of the Crusading army as they crossed the frozen lake. Here, Mongol or Turkish horse archers and cavalry attack the Danish contingent on the left flank of the Crusading force. (Angus McBride © Osprey Publishing)

HAKATA BAY, 1281

In 1206 the great Mongol leader Genghis Khan invaded the Chinese Empire. The Imperial capital of Peking was captured in 1215, and three years later the Mongol Horde reached Korea. In 1231 Korea would officially become a dependency of the Mongol Empire. These initial campaigns were followed by further expansion westwards, and the consolidation through conquest of the remainder of China. By 1279 the last resistance was overcome, as Genghis' successor Kublai Khan proclaimed himself Chinese Emperor, and founded the Yuan dynasty to rule what had effectively become a vast Mongol successor state. His real achievement, though, was to unite China into his sprawling empire to form a single political entity. However,

he still wished to expand his empire and in 1266 Kublai sent emissaries to the Japanese emperor to demand he become the Mongol's vassal. When these demands were ignored, Kublai Khan began planning to invade Japan.

In November 1274 a vast Mongol fleet made landfall in Hakata Bay (Hakata-Ku) in the Fukuoka province of the southerly Japanese island of Kyushu. On the way the Mongols had secured control of the islands of Tsushima and Iki. On landing, though, the Mongol beachhead was attacked by a Japanese army, and the two sides fought each other to a stalemate. The Mongols withdrew to their ships to regroup, at which point an unexpected storm swept over the region and half the fleet was sunk. The survivors of the invasion force withdrew to Korea.

Kublai Khan was determined to prevail and a second invasion force was assembled, in both Korea and Southern China. The attack was launched in early 1281, and again Tsushima and Iki were captured to protect the Mongols' lines of communication. As before, the 'Eastern Route' Mongol fleet from Korea arrived off Hakata Bay in early July, while a second diversionary landing was made at nearby Nagato,

on Kyushu, the Japanese mainland but was easily driven off. The shore at Hakata had been heavily fortified since the last invasion; therefore, the Mongols found landing there too hazardous. Instead, they withdrew to nearby islands to decide how best to proceed. The sensible course was to wait for the arrival of the 'Southern Route' fleet from China, and then to make an overwhelming combined assault.

The Japanese harried the Mongol fleet with small-scale raids, and recaptured the island of Iki. By then the two Mongol fleets had combined, and the Mongol commander, Arakhan, began his landing at Hakata Bay in early August. The Japanese defenders, though, were just as skilled, and managed to contain the bridgehead; the land campaign had reached a stalemate. Then, on 15 August, a major typhoon struck the Mongol fleet and most of its ships were wrecked. As the survivors struggled ashore they were killed by the waiting Japanese. The invasion was over and Japan had been saved from invasion. This ensured the continued independence of Japan, even though the victory owed as much to the weather as it did to the ferocity of the Japanese themselves.

LEFT In 1274, when the Mongols landed at Hakata Bay, they were met by unexpectedly tough resistance from the waiting Japanese samurai. The two sides fought each other to a standstill, prompting the battered Mongols to withdraw to their waiting ships to regroup. (Richard Hook © Osprey Publishing)

BANNOCKBURN, 23–24 JUNE 1314

In 1286 the accidental death of King Alexander III of Scotland plunged his kingdom into two decades of turmoil. The English King Edward I intervened to adjudicate the succession, installing a malleable ruler, and then when he rebelled Edward seized control of his kingdom. When William Wallace led a rebellion, Edward crushed it, and executed the patriot leader in 1305.

Scotland remained firmly under English control. However, a new leader arose, Robert the Bruce, Earl of Carrick, who had a good claim to the Scottish throne. He was crowned King Robert I of Scotland in early 1306. When Robert's small rebel force was scattered he waged a guerrilla war against the English occupiers. His family were imprisoned and his lands confiscated.

Robert's guerrilla campaign gathered pace after the death of Edward I, whose successor Edward II lacked his father's military acumen. Over the next few years Robert and his followers captured most of the English-held castles in Scotland, and by the start of 1314 only Stirling Castle remained. In response, Edward II gathered a large army in northern England, and that summer he marched north to relieve Stirling. At first, his advance was unopposed, but as he approached Stirling he found Robert's army blocking his path.

King Robert had around 7,500 men under his command, most of whom were spearmen. His small force of 500 cavalry was held in reserve. Edward had about 18,000 men, including an impressive array of 5,000 mounted men-at-arms, supported by archers and spearmen. The battle was fought over two days. On the first, 23 June, the two forces faced each other across a small stream, the Bannockburn, and the English vanguard attacked before the rest of the army could come up to support them. The attackers were disordered by lines of pits dug in front of the Scottish spearmen. The Scottish 'shiltrons' – dense blocks of spearmen – held firm, and the English were repulsed. At one stage the English knight Henry de Bohun challenged King Robert to single combat, but the Scots king avoided his assailant's lance, and then killed de Bohun with his axe. Then an attempt by 300 English men-at-arms to reach the castle was foiled by another shiltron and the knights were forced to retreat.

The real battle, though, took place the following day. The English army had camped on the flat lands to the east of the previous day's battlefield. At dawn Robert's army formed up and advanced towards them in a bristling line of spearpoints. The English knights charged repeatedly, but all their attacks were driven off. The swampy ground on their flanks prevented them from encircling the Scots, and so they were unable to take advantage of their superiority in numbers. The Scots cavalry drove off the unsupported English archers, who were Edward's only means of breaking the Scottish shiltrons. The English army became increasingly disordered, and when they saw what they thought was Scots reinforcements appearing they broke and ran. In fact it was Robert's camp followers, eager to be in 'at the kill'. Although Edward escaped, around half of his army were slaughtered or captured, including as many as 1,200 men-at-arms. Scots losses were considerably fewer. Bannockburn was the deciding moment of the Scottish Wars of Independence. The bloody victory at Bannockburn had secured King Robert's throne, and Scotland's independence.

LEFT The battle was decided on its second day, when increasingly desperate charges by the English mounted knights failed to break the dense ranks of the Scottish spearmen. Then the Scots began driving the English back towards their camp, and English resistance collapsed. (Graham Turner © Osprey Publishing)

THE BATTLE OF KULIKOVO, 1380

The Mongol invasion of China in the early 13th century was followed by an equally dramatic sweep through Central Asia into Eastern Europe. By 1240 the Kievan Rus' had been conquered, and the Mongol Horde swept on into Poland and Hungary. But the Mongols were checked at the Battle of Liegnitz (1241), and following the death of Ogodei Khan, son of the great Genghis Khan, the horde withdrew to the east to elect a new leader. The Mongol Empire then fragmented into several khanates. The most westerly of these was the Ulug Ulus, or Golden Horde, whose heartland was centred on the lower River Volga. On its northern boundaries the various Russian principalities paid tribute to the Horde to ensure their safety. By 1350 the largest of these was the

Grand Duchy of Moscow, whose capital had developed into an important political, religious and mercantile centre. The Princes of Moscow also acted as the khanate's tribute collectors among the Russian principalities.

Moscow's survival, though, still depended on the goodwill of the Golden Horde. By then these successors of the Mongol Empire were generally termed Tartars, a term reflecting the increasing Turkic influence in the Mongol khanate. The mid-14th century was marked by increasing internal strife within the Golden Horde, which encouraged the Muscovite rulers to consider ending the paying of tribute to the Tartars. However, it was 1378 before the Prince of Moscow Dmitri Ivanovich 'Donskoi' felt confident enough to take up arms against the Tartars. That year he attacked and defeated a small Tartar army at the Vozha River near Riazan. Mamai, the Horde's leading general, gathered an army to deal with the Muscovites.

It was Prince Dmitri who acted first, though, leading his Russian army south along the banks of the River Don into Tartar territory. The two armies met at Kulikovo, some 50 miles southeast of Tula. Numbers are uncertain, but Dmitri probably commanded around 30,000–50,000 men, a mixture of infantry and cavalry, while Mamai's army was a little larger, and was markedly superior in cavalry. To avoid being encircled, Dmitri anchored his right flank on the River Nepryadva, a tributary of the Don, and his left on a wood. Mamai attacked almost immediately, his cavalry overwhelming the infantry of the first Russian line. Dmitri was stationed with the reserve, so one of his nobles, Michael Brenk, coordinated the battle for him. The Russian cavalry and infantry reserve then counter-attacked, and a furious melee developed, which would last for almost three hours.

Both sides fed in their last reserves of troops, but it was the Russians who made the decisive blow, unleashing a force of cavalry which until now had been hidden in the wood. It fell on the Tartar rear, and Mamai's exhausted army wavered, then broke. The day ended in a Russian victory, but the cost had been immense, with both sides losing almost half of their army in the fight. This victory didn't lead to Russian independence from the Tartars – that would take another century – but it signalled the decline of the Golden Horde, and marked the coming of age of Muscovy.

LEFT A key point in the battle came when the Golden Horde's commander Mamai attempted to kill the leader he thought was the Russian Prince Dmitri 'Donskoi'. Instead his cavalry attacked a 'false Dmitri', leaving the real prince free to unleash his own counter-attack. (Darren Tan © Osprey Publishing)

THE BATTLE OF TANNENBERG, 15 JULY 1410

From the early 13th century, militant Christian Orders had embarked on a 'Northern Crusade' to enforce a Latin version of Christianity on the 'pagan' Baltic tribes. These crusades lasted for two centuries, as the Teutonic and Livonian Orders campaigned against the Prussians and Lithuanians. By the mid-14th century the increasingly powerful Kingdom of Poland had become resentful of the military orders, and although Christian themselves, they began to openly side with the Lithuanians. In 1370 the Teutonic Order defeated the Lithuanians at the Battle of Rudau, fought near modern-day Kaliningrad. This ultimately led to the Christianisation of Lithuania, which in turn paved the diplomatic way for a Polish-Lithuanian

union, which was formally agreed in the Union of Krewo (1385). This union would last for another four centuries. To cement this bond, the following year the Lithuanian Grand Duke Jagiello became King Wyadislaw II of Poland.

However, this didn't stop the Teutonic Order's military campaigns against Lithuania, which continued intermittently until a peace treaty was signed in 1401, brokered by Wyadislaw's brother Grand Duke Vytautas, who ruled Lithuania on his behalf. However, in 1409 the brothers incited unrest in Samogitia, a northern Lithuanian province which had been seized by the Teutonic Order. The Order's Grand Master Ulrich von Jungingen duly declared war on both Poland and Lithuania. The brothers decided to unite their forces, then march on the Order's capital of Marienburg (now Malbork in Poland). Although numbers are uncertain, Jungingen commanded around 20,000 men, most of whom were cavalry, while the Polish-Lithuanian army was larger, around 35,000 strong. Vytautas had operational command of the army on the battlefield.

In early July the allies marched into Prussia, and after initial skirmishing around the Masurian Lakes the two armies met near the villages of Tannenberg (now Stębark) and Grünwald in what is now northern Poland. On the morning of 15 July the battle began with a Teutonic cannonade. This goaded the Lithuanian cavalry into charging the guns, but they were counter-charged by the Teutonic cavalry who put them to flight. The Order's cavalry continued to pursue the Lithuanians, but found themselves isolated by the Poles, who advanced to engage the Order's centre. A fiercely fought melee followed, which eventually saw the Teutonic troops pushed back.

The Grand Master committed his reserves to strengthen his line, but Wyadislaw did the same, using his Polish reserves to fall on the Order's right flank. At that point Vytautas' Lithuanians, having rallied on the shores of Lake Lubicz, advanced again and fell on the left flank and rear of the Grand Master's army, which was virtually surrounded. Resistance collapsed when Jungingen fell, although the slaughter continued until nightfall. The battle effectively ended the Teutonic Order, as most of their army was either killed or captured. Allied losses were around 5,000–6,000. The battle ended the risk of an annexation of the region by the Crusading Order, and so helped secure the continued independence of Poland and Lithuania. It also marked the start of the Polish-Lithuanian union as a dominant power in Eastern Europe.

LEFT The attack by Grand Master von Jungingen was halted by the cavalry of the Polish King Wyadislaw II, who then used his greater numbers to surround his adversaries. The death of Jungingen at around 2pm led to the slaughter of the remaining Teutonic knights. (Richard Hook © Osprey Publishing)

THE BATTLE OF AGINCOURT, 25 OCTOBER 1415

In 1337 England and France embarked on a war, fought over the feudal relationships between the countries' kings, as the French monarch considered his English counterpart to be his vassal. Dubbed the Hundred Years War, the struggle lasted for 116 years (1337–1453). It was fought intermittently, and what began as a feudal dispute developed into a national one, beginning a rivalry that would last for half a millennium. In the mid-14th century, the English achieved several notable victories over the French, at Sluys (1340), Crécy (1346) and Poitiers (1356). These victories were largely due to the skill

of the English longbowmen, whose skill in archery was widely recognized in medieval Europe.

However, English victories won on the battlefield were countered by French success in capturing and retaining territory. So the war dragged on intermittently, with neither side able to achieve victory. Eventually an uneasy truce was arranged in 1396, which lasted for 17 years. In 1413 the accession of the warlike Henry V to the English throne marked the end of this. His diplomatic moves to isolate France angered the new French king Charles VI, and a renewal of the war became inevitable. On 12 August 1415 Henry landed at Harfleur in Normandy, and besieged the port with an army of 12,000 men. It fell five weeks later, but the operation had cost Henry almost 2,000 men through death or disease. He now lacked the men he needed to continue his conquests.

After garrisoning Harfleur, Henry marched overland to English-held Calais, planning to renew the campaign the following spring. He set off on 10 October, but his march was hampered by bad weather. Meanwhile, King Charles had amassed an army of 60,000 men near the River Somme. Henry, though, found an unguarded crossing on 19 October, and continued on towards Calais. However, he was shadowed by the French and five days later Henry decided to stand and fight. He had around 6,000 men; around 1,200 billmen and men-at-arms, a small mounted reserve, and the rest longbowmen. Charles' army, commanded by the Dukes of Bourbon and Orléans, contained about 12,000 mounted men-at-arms, supported by spearmen, crossbowmen and hangers-on. Amid heavy rain, the two sides deployed astride the Calais road near the village of Agincourt.

Henry's little army was drawn up between two woods. He interspersed his men-at-arms amid his blocks of archers, their front protected by wooden stakes. The French deployed in three deep mixed divisions of crossbowmen, spearmen and cavalry. Given the woods, this would be a frontal assault. At 11am that morning, when the French had not made any move, Henry ordered his archers forward to harry the French lines. This goaded them into a wild assault, spearheaded by the cavalry. The longbowmen ran back through their stakes, and slaughtered the French in droves, while the charging cavalry were unable to find a way through the stakes, and floundered in the mud.

The bodies piled up, making it even harder for the French to break through. Many were captured, and Henry ordered most of them killed, as nobody could be spared to guard them. Eventually the third French division refused to charge, and began to flee the field. Against the odds Henry had emerged victorious. Over 7,000 French died or were captured that day, while Henry lost less than 600 men. Henry and his men returned to England as heroes, and when they returned to France they would return to conquer.

LEFT At Agincourt the attack on the English lines by the dismounted French men-at-arms ended in slaughter as the French nobles were slowed by the cloying mud, and then hit by a storm of arrows. The English then sallied out from their lines to finish off the French survivors. (Graham Turner © Osprey Publishing)

CONSTANTINOPLE, 1453

Their defeat at the Battle of Manzikert in 1071 marked the end of Byzantine aspirations to further military glory, but the Empire survived, despite a steady erosion of its power and wealth. Since its rebranding from Byzantium in AD 330, Constantinople had remained at the heart of this decaying empire and had only been captured once, in 1204. Ironically this was at the hands of fellow Christians during the Fourth Crusade, who held the city until it was recaptured by the Byzantines in 1261. The Crusaders also claimed swathes of Byzantine territory for themselves, forming semi-independent Latin states in Greece, while other parts of the Empire became increasingly autonomous. Somehow, though, the decaying Empire managed to struggle on in the

face of repeated attacks by Turkish, Latin and Balkan invaders.

It was the Turks, though, who presented the greatest threat, and by 1450 they had conquered almost all of Asia Minor. By then, all that remained of the Empire were a few scattered provinces in Greece, the Aegean, and on the fringe of the Black Sea. Then, in 1451, a teenager succeeded his father as Sultan of the Ottoman Turks, becoming Mehmed II. He would soon earn the cognomen of 'the Conqueror'. When he gained the throne he began preparing to attack Constantinople by building a fleet and a powerful siege train. He also gained control of both sides of the Bosphorus, covering the channel with his fleet and two forts. Effectively, this meant Constantinople was now isolated.

Knowing what was coming, the Byzantine emperor Constantine XI asked the European states for help, but very few reinforcements arrived before Constantinople was invested. The city's 12-mile circuit of walls was garrisoned by around 6,000 men – a tenth of the Ottoman army that appeared on the landward side of the city in early April 1453. A Turkish fleet of 110 galleys blockaded the seaward side. On 12 April the siege began with lengthy artillery bombardment. One of these Turkish 'bombards' fired stone balls weighing almost half a ton. After six days of this the city's outer walls had been breached, and on 18 April Mehmed launched the first of several assaults. Each of them, though, was repulsed. During early May an attempt to mine the walls failed, as did further attacks on the breaches, which had been partly shored up. The Turkish army was growing restless, but Mehmed insisted on one final assault. For two days his guns opened up a continual bombardment, then, at 11.30am on 29 May, the sultan unleashed his whole army against the walls. At first the defenders held their ground, but then a party of attackers found a small open gate and they surged in. The defences had been breached. With that, Mehmed unleashed his elite guard, the Janissaries, and the last pockets of resistance were overcome. The Turks then surged into the city, and an orgy of violence and destruction followed. The Byzantine Empire had fallen, and Constantinople has remained a Muslim city ever since.

LEFT During the final Turkish assault on Constantinople the Byzantines successfully held the walls, until the attackers found a way into the city and so bypassed the defences. With the fall of his city inevitable, Emperor Constantine died, sword in hand, surrounded by his foes. (Christa Hook © Osprey Publishing)

CASTILLON, 17 JULY 1453

After his victory at Agincourt in 1415, Henry V would return to systematically conquer most of northern France, including Paris, while retaining the English hold on Gascony and Guyenne, to the south and east of Bordeaux. French fortunes were at a low ebb, but in 1429 the situation improved, largely due to the emergence of Joan of Arc, a peasant girl who convinced the French that God favoured them. Largely thanks to her the key city of Orléans was recaptured, and a resurgent France embraced a new-found spirit of nationalism. Joan was captured by the English in 1430 and executed for heresy the following year, but her influence continued to inspire the French, who went on to recapture Paris in 1436. In 1444 a five-year peace was negotiated, and

King Charles VII used this time to reorganize the French Army along more professional lines.

When the fighting resumed in 1449, the French embarked on a reconquest of Normandy, capturing the key city of Rouen on the Seine, then decisively defeating the English at the Battle of Formigny (1450). That left the province open to the French, who went on to capture Caen and Cherbourg. The fall of the port in August 1450 marked an end to English rule in Normandy. The French then turned their attention to Gascony. In the spring of 1451 the French Count of Dunois invaded Guyenne with a small army, accompanied by a sizeable artillery train. In June he used these guns to capture Bordeaux, and two months later Bayonne fell to the French. After three centuries of English rule, though, the local nobles opposed the French invasion, and begged King Henry VI of England for help. In response, a small English army led by the elderly John Talbot, Earl of Shrewsbury, landed near Bordeaux the following October. The port city opened its gates to him, and so it returned to English hands.

That winter, as Shrewsbury reclaimed much of the region, both sides prepared for a fresh campaign in the spring. In May 1453, three French columns entered Guyenne from the north and east and converged on Bordeaux. In early July they laid siege to the town of Castillon on the Dordogne, 25 miles east of Bordeaux. In mid-July Shrewsbury marched out of the port to relieve Castillon, and on 17 July his vanguard of 1,200 mounted troops overran a French outpost in a priory, protecting their siege lines around the town. Then, instead of waiting for reinforcements, Shrewsbury saw dust clouds, and assumed the French Army was retreating, so he pressed on, hoping to captured the train of French guns before they could be towed away. Instead, when he arrived in front of the main French camp he found the enemy's lines were fully manned.

Undeterred he ordered an immediate assault on the French siege camp. Its defence was coordinated by Jean Bureau, King Charles' Master of Artillery, who had turned his guns around to defend the camp. The assault was broken by gunfire, and both Shrewsbury and his son Lord Lisle were killed in the counter-attack that followed. Over 4,000 of their men were slaughtered with them, while French casualties were minimal. With the fall of Bordeaux that October, Calais became England's last possession on French soil. Castillon was the last major battle of the Hundred Years War.

LEFT The height of the battle came when the English launched an all-out assault on the defences of the French artillery park. The defenders hung on, though, until Breton cavalry arrived, which charged into the flank of the English force, killing John Talbot and routing his army. (Graham Turner © Osprey Publishing)

BOSWORTH, 22 AUGUST 1485

Historians disagree over why the Wars of the Roses began, but at their heart was the mentally infirm King Henry VI, of the Lancastrian dynasty, whose ineffectual reign encouraged the revolt of the rival claimants to the throne from the house of York. The king's cousin Richard of York rose in revolt in 1455, and for the next 30 years England was riven by a bloody civil war.

The fortunes of York and Lancaster waxed and waned, but Henry was eventually killed, and Richard's son Edward acceded to the throne. Then, in 1483, Richard of York's second son succeeded his brother, and was duly crowned Richard III.

The murders of the two 'Princes in the Tower', his brother Edward's rightful heirs, did little for

Richard's popularity, though, and this encouraged a new claimant to enter the royal ring. Henry Tudor, the son of Henry VI's half-brother, assembled 1,800 French mercenaries in Harfleur, and then in August 1485 he landed in the Welsh port of Milford Haven. He rallied Welsh supporters to his cause, and then marched into England, attracting more support along the way. By the time he reached Shrewsbury he had 5,000 men at his back, including several English nobles. Meanwhile King Richard gathered his army at Leicester. The two armies drew closer as Henry marched east through Staffordshire, and on 21 August he came upon Richard's army of 7,900 men encamped on Ambion Hill near Market Bosworth.

The following day, Richard deployed his army for battle. He commanded the central 'battle' (or division), with the battles of the Duke of Norfolk on his right and the Earl of Northumberland on his left. A fourth force of 4,000 men under Lord Stanley kept its distance, though, despite demands from the king. Stanley wanted to see how the battle developed before committing his troops. As was the case throughout the Wars of the Roses, the rival armies were made up of longbowmen, supported by billmen and either mounted or dismounted men-at-arms. Henry Tudor, though, also had his French mercenaries, armed with pikes and crossbows. His army was grouped in one large battle commanded by the Earl of Oxford, while Henry accompanied a smaller reserve commanded by his kinsman Jasper Tudor.

Richard watched Henry deploy his force below the hill, then after handing over his battle to his deputy, the Duke of Norfolk, he ordered both his own and Norfolk's battle to advance. Richard and his mounted bodyguard, and Northumberland's battle remained on the hill. Despite being outnumbered, Oxford's men held their ground, and the fight at the foot of the hill devolved into a brutal close-quarters melee. When Richard spotted Henry, he led a cavalry charge against him. That was when Stanley made his move, leading his men into the fight – and attacking King Richard. This proved the tipping point of the battle. Unhorsed, Richard was cut down almost within sword-reach of Henry Tudor. With the king dead, his army broke and ran, pursued by the victorious Tudors and Stanleys. Casualties were slight, though, with Richard's army losing around 1,000 men, including the king and Norfolk, and Henry's force losing considerably fewer. Henry Tudor – soon to be Henry VII, and father of Henry VIII – had won a kingdom. Save for one last rebellion two years later, Bosworth also brought the tempestuous Wars of the Roses to a close.

LEFT At Bosworth, Richard III had been watching the battle develop, but when he spotted Henry Tudor he led his mounted men-at-arms forward to attack him. However, in the melee that followed Richard was surrounded by his opponents, and was unhorsed and hacked to death. (Graham Turner © Osprey Publishing)

THE RENAISSANCE

TENOCHTITLAN, MAY–AUGUST 1521

For two centuries, from *c.*1325 on, the Aztec emperors had ruled over an empire of five million subjects and their allies in Central and southern North America. This empire – really a confederation of semi-autonomous cities and regions – was one of the most advanced and prosperous cultures in the Americas, rivalled only by the great Incan Empire of South America. Aztec society was bound together by religion and war – the two linked inextricably together as the religious demand for human sacrifices required a steady stream of prisoners, captured during the near-incessant wars with neighbouring peoples. From his capital of Tenochtitlan (now Mexico City), built in the centre of Lake Texcoco, the Aztec emperor

Montezuma II was the undisputed master of Central America. This changed forever in early 1519, when the Spanish conquistador Hernán Cortés (1485–1547) and 600 of his men landed on the coast of Mexico.

After founding a settlement he called Vera Cruz, Cortés marched inland, towards the Aztec capital he had heard so much about. As he went he subdued the Aztecs' allies, then ensured they switched their allegiance to him. On 8 November he and his conquistadors entered Tenochtitlan unopposed by advancing up one of the lake causeways leading to the city. When he met Montezuma, it became clear that the Aztecs regarded Cortés as a god. For the moment this ensured the conquistadors were safe, but Cortés knew they were surrounded by a potentially hostile people, and so took steps to ensure his men's safety. He captured Montezuma, as by holding him hostage he hoped to ensure the acquiescence of the Aztec people.

The following April, another conquistador, Pánfilo de Narváez, landed in Vera Cruz with orders for Cortés' recall. Cortés responded by attacking and capturing his rival, whom he held prisoner for the next two years. When Cortés returned to Tenochtitlan, though, he found the Aztecs had revolted. When Cortés used Montezuma to placate his own people, the Aztecs stoned the emperor, and Montezuma died of his wounds. The situation deteriorated fast, and so on 30 June 1520 the conquistadors fought their way out of the city along a causeway and withdrew to the friendly city of Tlaxcala. Cortés had lost half of his men, but he was determined to regain control of the Aztec capital. Thus, in May 1521 he led his men to the shore of Lake Texcoco, and began assembling the squadron of 13 small prefabricated sailing boats his men had built over the winter. He had 900 Spaniards at his command including 90 cavalrymen, and 18 small guns, plus some Tlaxcalan allies.

In May, Cortés blockaded the three causeways into the city, then used his gun-armed brigantines to bombard the city. The Aztecs tried to attack them in canoes, but these were all sunk by gunfire. The boats then fired at any Aztec columns trying to escape along the causeways. This unusual siege lasted for 93 days, until the conquistadores advanced into the city and cleared it block by block. Over 40,000 Aztecs were killed before the city finally fell on 13 August. For the next three centuries, Tenochtitlan, now Mexico City, would be the capital of 'New Spain'.

LEFT Having been trapped in Tenochtitlan when the Aztecs rose in revolt, Cortés and his men stormed the immense Temple of Yopico, hoping to turn it into a defensible fortress. It soon became clear, though, that the Spaniards had little choice but to abandon the city entirely. (Peter Dennis © Osprey Publishing)

PAVIA, 24 FEBRUARY 1525

In 1494, when the French king Charles VIII invaded Italy, he began a conflict that would last for half a century. His invasion had been an attempt to reinforce a minor dynastic claim to the throne of Naples, but it soon developed into a major struggle between France and Imperial Spain, the two superpowers of 16th-century Europe. Renaissance Italy became a battleground, as its republics and city states sided with one power or the other in a bid for their own survival. Military successes on both sides were followed by equally critical defeats. As a result, the fortunes of war remained in the balance. This, though, would change at the Battle of Pavia.

In early 1515, King Francis I succeeded to the French throne, and reinvigorated the French

cause. That autumn he captured Milan, after defeating the Milanese army and its Swiss mercenaries at the Battle of Marignano. This key Italian city remained in French hands until its capture by an Imperialist army of Germans and Spaniards six years later. When the French tried to recapture Milan in April 1522, their army of mercenary Swiss pikemen was defeated at the Battle of Bicocca. The French had now been driven out of Italy, but Francis was determined to regain control of Milan, which he saw as the key to northern Italy, so he raised a new, larger army, which he intended to lead in person.

However, in 1523–24 Francis' advanced guard was manoeuvred out of Italy by the new Imperialist commander, Charles de Lannoy. The Imperialists then raided Provence and besieged Marseilles, before being chased out of France by Francis at the head of a larger French army. In September Francis pursued them and went on to recapture Milan. Now, with more Imperialist troops massing, he had to hold on to his gains. Therefore, in late October he laid siege to Pavia, a city south of Milan which was garrisoned by the Imperialists. Pavia was still holding out, though, when an Imperialist relief force arrived in early February. It established its own earthworks; the besiegers had become the besieged. Lannoy's Imperialist army of 24,000 men included German Landsknecht pikemen, Spanish and Italian arquebusiers, Spanish and German men-at-arms and Spanish and Italian light cavalry. Francis' army was of a similar size, and included Swiss and Landsknecht pikemen, French and Italian arquebusiers and elite French gendarmes, as well as light cavalry.

The bulk of Francis' army was deployed in a hunting park to the north of the city. At dawn on 24 February Lannoy's troops broke into it, and fell upon the scattered French garrison. In the south-east park corner, Imperialist Landsknechts fought French-paid Swiss pikemen, and eventually defeated them. To the west, Francis' main force was attacked by Spanish and German troops, but his gendarmes drove off the Imperialist cavalry. The gendarmes and the French-paid Landsknechts were outflanked, though, and were eventually routed. In the struggle Francis was unhorsed and captured. The French lost around 8,000 men killed or captured that morning, including their king. Francis was ransomed and freed, but Italy was lost, and a peace was signed in 1529 which brought the long and hard-fought war to an end.

LEFT During the morning assault on the French camp, while part of the attackers engaged the French gendarmes and Swiss pikemen, half of the Imperialist commander Georg von Frundsberg's Landsknechts fought the Black Band, Landsknechts in French service, in a bitter fight to the death. (Graham Turner © Osprey Publishing)

CUZCO, 1536–37

Before the arrival of the Spanish the Incan Empire had flourished on the western side of the Andes for almost three centuries. By the early 16th century it was regarded as one of the world's great civilizations. It boasted a relatively sophisticated level of technical and cultural advancement, and its emperor held power over seven million subjects thanks to his state's highly developed civil service and considerable financial and administrative resources. It also had a large and comparatively powerful army. It would be speedily conquered, though, by the Spanish conquistador Francisco Pizarro, and 200 men. Pizarro had accompanied other Spanish expeditions, including Vasco Núñez de Balboa's one to Panama in 1513 which first sighted the

Pacific Ocean. In 1526, however, Pizarro first came into contact with the northern fringes of the Incan Empire.

Pizarro returned in 1531 at the head of his small body of conquistadors to find the Empire was riven by a war of succession between two Incan princes, Huascar and Atahualpa. He turned this to his advantage by pursuing a policy of 'divide and conquer'. When he encountered Atahualpa, Pizarro captured the prince before his vast army could react. Atahualpa was duly ransomed for a room filled with gold and silver. Word then reached Pizarro that Huascar had been poisoned, so the Incan Empire was now leaderless. Therefore, in July 1532 he kept the ransom but executed Atahualpa anyway, and then marched south to seize the rest of the Incan Empire. Ironically, the superb Incan network of roads greatly accelerated the fall of the empire. After the Incan capital of Cuzco was captured in November 1533, it was simply a matter of mopping up.

Pizarro installed a puppet emperor, Manco Inca Yupanqui, but the Spanish treated him with such contempt that in April 1536 the Incan escaped from Cuzco and began raising an army. When Pizarro marched south to deal with it, his 190 Spaniards were faced with an force of 100,000 or more warriors. The Spanish wisely withdrew to Cuzco, and in May they were duly besieged by Manco Inca's immense army. Pizarro did what he could to fortify the city, and to disorder the besiegers. In mid-May he sent his brother Juan and 50 cavalry to seize the nearby walled town of Sacsayhumán, which the Incans used as a depot. However, in the fight for the town Juan was wounded by a slingshot, and later died of his wounds. Sacsayhumán was captured, but at a great personal cost to Pizarro.

Three weeks later a small body of Spanish reinforcements approached Cuzco from Lima, Pizarro's newly founded capital. The small column was ambushed by the Incans and killed, and Manco sent a detachment north to capture and burn the now lightly protected capital. In January Pizarro led another sortie against Manco's headquarters at Ollantaytambo but was repulsed. Conditions inside Cuzco were now desperate. However, in March Manco lifted the siege as a powerful Spanish relief force led by Diego del Almagro was approaching. The two conquistadors would soon fall out, and would fight for control of what was now Peru, as Manco and his dwindling band resorted to guerrilla warfare, but were ultimately unable to regain their lost empire.

LEFT When Francisco Pizarro offered to meet the Incan prince Atahualpa in the town of Cajamarca, the conquistadors ambushed the emperor's escort, slaying them and capturing their ruler. This paralysed the Incan Empire, allowing Pizarro to claim it all for himself. (Giuseppe Rava © Osprey Publishing)

MALTA, MAY–SEPTEMBER 1565

After its capture of Constantinople in 1453 the Ottoman Turkish Empire extended its influence through much of the Middle East and the Balkans, and along the North African coast, where the piratical city states of Tunis and Algiers recognized Turkish suzerainty. With the capture of Baghdad in 1534, Sultan Suleiman I 'the Magnificent' was free to turn westwards. His defeat of King Louis II of Hungary at the Battle of Mohács in 1526 had secured his hold over the Balkans, but a further advance on Vienna was thwarted. However, from 1530 on it was the Mediterranean that would prove the key battle ground between Turks and Christians.

For years the Knights of St. John on Rhodes had acted as a bastion against Turkish expansion.

After the fall of the island stronghold in 1522, this sea-based Christian Order re-established itself in Malta. Now, as the Ottomans and their Barbary allies raided into the Central and Western Mediterranean, the Knights of St. John were once again at the forefront of the struggle. For decades they and the Barbary pirates had fought each other for control of the Western Mediterranean's sea lanes. From 1530 on, the greatly expanded Ottoman navy ventured into the Adriatic and the Central Mediterranean, and brief attacks on Malta, Corfu and Calabria followed. There were naval clashes too; in 1538 the Ottoman fleet was defeated at Prevesa off the Greek Adriatic coast, while the Barbary pirates defeated the Christians off Djerba in modern-day Tunisia in 1560. After that Christian setback, it was evident that Malta would be the Ottoman sultan's next target.

Sure enough, on 18 May 1565 a combined Ottoman and Barbary fleet of almost 200 galleys and transport ships arrived off Malta, and disembarked an army of almost 40,000 men. The 6,000 defenders withdrew to the island's heavily fortified Grand Harbour, and the Turks followed, establishing their siege lines on 21 May. A hasty initial assault was repulsed, so Turgut (or Dragut) Reis, the Barbary leader of the army, turned his attention to Fort St. Elmo, which lay across the harbour from the main town of Birgu. After a lengthy artillery bombardment the fort was finally taken on 23 June, after a bloody assault. However, this had cost the lives of 6,000 Turks, including Turgut Reis. Mustafa Pasha then assumed command of the army.

Attention now turned to Birgu itself, protected by the Castel St. Angelo, and the neighbouring fortified peninsula of Senglea. Turkish artillery bombarded the defences, while Mustafa prepared a seaborne assault on Senglea. It was thwarted, though, by a line of obstacles, and a probe was driven off by Christian gunfire. Then, on 15 July, the Turks exploded a mine underneath Senglea's outer defences. Turkish troops stormed the breach, but were repulsed after heavy fighting and a counter-attack by the Knights' Grand Master, Jean de Valette. The non-stop bombardment continued, but other attacks also faltered. In early September Mustafa broke off the siege, and planned to winter in Malta, before resuming the siege the following year. However, the landing of a Christian relief force encouraged Mustafa to retreat to his ships and abandon the siege. Malta had been spared, and the Ottoman expansion into the Western Mediterranean had been thwarted.

LEFT During the siege of Malta the Ottoman Turks concentrated their efforts on St. Elmo's Fort, which guarded the approaches to the harbour. Once the Turkish guns opened a breach the fort was stormed and captured, and most of the Knights of St. John defending it were slain. (Christa Hook © Osprey Publishing)

LEPANTO, 7 OCTOBER 1571

Some historians claim the Great Siege of Malta in 1565 represented the high-water mark of Ottoman expansion. However, this view ignores the powerful Ottoman galley fleet, which together with its Barbary corsair allies still dominated the waters of the Central Mediterranean. The death of Suleiman 'the Magnificent' in 1566 was more of a watershed, as his son Selim II 'the Sot' lacked his father's appetite for military conquest. Instead, he lived up to his epithet, and left his Grand Vizier Mehmed Pasha to run his empire for him. Four years after the siege of Malta the Barbary corsairs drove the Spanish from Tunis, and so were able to renew their raids on the coast of southern Italy. In the Eastern Mediterranean, the Turks

successfully drove the Venetians from Cyprus in 1570–71. They then concentrated their fleet at Lepanto on the Greek coast of the Adriatic, to isolate the Venetian-held island of Crete.

The Christian response to this was the establishment of a Holy League, which incorporated most of the Christian powers. Its military power, though, was concentrated in its fleet of more than 200 galleys, supplied by Spain, Venice, the Papal States, the Knights of St. John and other smaller maritime powers. Its commander was Don Juan of Austria, the illegitimate son of the Holy Roman Emperor Charles V. It would face an Ottoman Turkish fleet of around 250 galleys, under the command of Müezzinzade Ali Pasha. This fleet included a sizeable Barbary contingent led by Uluç Ali Pasha. In late September 1571 the Christian fleet arrived off the island of Corfu, then cruised south towards the Gulf of Corinth. The Turkish commanders decided to give battle, and on the morning of 7 October the two fleets met off the entrance of the gulf, near the small port of Lepanto (now Nafpactos).

The two fleets each deployed in three squadrons, which faced each other. The battle began shortly after 10am, as the galleys opened fire on each other. The northernmost squadrons were the first to clash, and a bitter hand-to-hand boarding action began which raged until the early afternoon. By then the Christians had gradually gained the upper hand. In the centre the two flagships clashed with each other, and the rival squadrons joined in, in a swirl of ramming, boarding and close-range gunfire. However, after two hours the Turkish flagship was captured and Ali Pasha was killed. With that his remaining ships broke off the fight, together with the northern Turkish squadron.

On the Christian right, their squadron tried to outflank the Barbary squadron, which avoided it and attacked the Christian centre instead. Uluç Ali fought well, but when Müezzinzade Ali Pasha was killed, and the southern Christian squadron reappeared, he too broke off the fight and escaped towards the open sea. This hard-fought galley battle ended a decisive victory for the Holy League. Some two-thirds of the Ottoman ships were sunk or captured, while the Christians lost 13 galleys. This, the greatest naval battle of the Renaissance, effectively ended any further Ottoman threat in the Mediterranean.

LEFT While most of the two fleets at Lepanto were made up of conventional galleys, the large Venetian contingent contained six galleasses, whose considerable firepower was used effectively to break up the Turkish line, and then to disrupt and delay the enemy reserves. (Tony Bryan © Osprey Publishing)

GRAVELINES, 1588

In 1558, Elizabeth I succeeded to the English throne, and while she remained at peace with Spain, King Philip II of Spain became increasingly irritated by her policies: supporting the Dutch in their revolt against Spanish rule; imprisoning the Catholic Mary, Queen of Scots; and investing in the ventures of English 'sea dogs' as they traded illegally in the Spanish New World. Following Elizabeth's excommunication by the Pope in 1570, the English queen openly encouraged English privateering against the Spanish. Finally, in 1585, when she signed a treaty of support with the Dutch, Philip II lost his patience. He ordered an invasion fleet to be gathered, to invade England and depose its troublesome Protestant queen.

In the summer of 1587 this Spanish 'Armada' began to assemble in Lisbon, and late the following May it finally set sail. The Armada consisted of 130 ships, most of which were armed merchantmen, but also a core of powerful galleons and other warships. This force was under the command of the Duke of Medina Sidonia. His plan was to sail up the English Channel, then embark an army of Spanish veterans at Dunkirk. These troops would then be transported to England. On 30 July the force arrived off the south-west coast of England, where Lord Howard of Effingham was waiting for it. His English fleet was made up of 34 royal warships, supported by over 160 armed merchantmen. On 31 July the two fleets clashed off Plymouth. This was the start of a running battle as the Spanish Armada made its way up the Channel.

The English were unable to break the Spaniards' defensive formation, and on 6 August the Armada dropped anchor off Calais. There Medina Sidonia waited for the Duke of Parma and his Spanish army to join him. However, during the night of 7–8 August the English sent fireships against the Spanish fleet, which was forced to scatter. At dawn the Spanish were to the north of the small port of Gravelines. As the Spanish ships tried to regroup, the English fleet closed for the attack. The fight that followed would last for most of the day. Unlike the running battle of the previous week, this was a close-range duel, with Medina Sidonia using his most powerful galleons to protect the rest of the fleet. His flagship *San Martin* was badly damaged, and by 10am she was forced to retreat inside a protective ring of other Spanish ships. In one way the Spanish were lucky – a portion of the English fleet was too busy trying to pillage a grounded Spanish warship, the *San Lorenzo*, and so missed most of the fighting. As the day wore on the Spanish fleet became increasingly battered, but Medina Sidonia, with a new rearguard, managed to keep his fleet together until nightfall. By then he had been driven out of sight of the coast, and so any chances of embarking a Spanish army had gone. Instead his fleet had been driven into the North Sea, and he was left with no alternative but to head for home, circumnavigating the British Isles as he went. Most of his damaged ships didn't make it, succumbing instead to the September gales and the rocky coast of Ireland. Elizabethan England had been saved, thanks more to nature, though, than to the English fleet.

LEFT The decisive action of the Spanish Armada campaign was fought off Gravelines. After the Armada was disordered by a night attack by fireships, the smaller English fleet harried them as the Spanish tried to re-form, their guns inflicting heavy damage on the enemy ships. (Tony Bryan © Osprey Publishing)

SEKIGAHARA, 1600

In theory Japan was a feudal state ruled by the emperor, who wielded total power. In practice, though, since before the Mongol Invasions of the late 13th century, imperial power had declined steadily, and increasingly power was vested in several great clans, ruled over by a warlord or Shogun. Their power rested in their samurai armies. During the *Sengoku* ('Warring States') period which began in 1467, the structure of this feudal society broke down amid civil war and clan feuds. During this time attempts were made to unify Japan under a single warlord, one of the most successful being Toyotomi Hideyoshi, *daimyo* ('feudal lord') of the powerful Toyotomi clan. Following his death in 1599 his son Hideyori was named as his successor, but as he

was only five years old the Shogunate was administered by five regents. Inevitably, some of them attempted to seize power for themselves.

One of these was Tokugawa Ieyasu, an influential and respected former ally of Hideyoshi. He gathered support for his bid for power from the clans of eastern Japan. Three of his rival regents sided with the *daimyo* Ishida Mitsunari, who gathered support from the Toyotomi clan, and from their many allies in western Japan. The country was therefore divided between two rival factions, or Eastern and Western armies, and a battle between them was now inevitable. The Western army gathered at Osaka Castle, and in the autumn of 1600 Ieyasu's Eastern army advanced towards it. On 21 October the two armies encountered each other at Sekigahara in Mino Province. Tokugawa Ieyasu had around 75,000 men at his command, while Ishida Mitsunari lay across his line of advance with a much larger army of up to 120,000 men.

Dense fog covered the battlefield that morning, and it was two hours before it cleared enough for both commanders to grasp exactly what was happening. The Tokugawa vanguard standing by the River Fuji charged into the defender's centre, and Ieyasu sent the rest of his army forward to support them. Command problems in the Western army meant that, at first, Ishida Mitsunari was unable to react to this. The fighting involved well-armed samurai on foot and horseback, spear-armed infantry and archers, and even a small number of arquebusiers and artillery. The Tokugawa assault was gaining ground, but a counter-attack could still have saved the day.

The moment passed when the *daimyo* Kobayakawa Hideaki switched sides. His 16,000 men holding the high ground of Mount Matsuo then charged into the flank of the Western samurai lord Ōtani Yoshitsugu, whose men were bearing the brunt of the Tokugawa assault. The defenders began to fall back, at which point several other groups within the Western army also began to switch sides. Thus, Ishida Mitsunari's large Western army disintegrated, as those factions which had remained loyal now found themselves outnumbered. Ishida Mitsunari was captured and executed after the battle, while Ōtani Yoshitsugu took his own life. Casualties were probably less than 10,000 men on each side. After the battle Tokugawa Ieyasu became the de facto ruler of Japan, and in 1604 the emperor named him Shogun. His Shogunate effectively ended the era of civil wars in Japan, and ushered in a lengthy era of national stability.

LEFT The great *daimyo* Tokugawa Ieyasu, his presence denoted through the mist by his clan banner and golden sun standard, watches the opening move of the battle, the charge of his vanguard, commanded by Ii Naomasa, who is shown here leading his 'Red Devil' samurai. (Giuseppe Rava © Osprey Publishing)

OSAKA, 1614–15

After the Battle of Sekigahara in 1600, the civil wars that had plagued feudal Japan during the Sengoku period came to an end. The Tokugawa clan became the dominant family in the country, and effectively ruled Japan from its new clan base in Edo Castle. This dominance was cemented in 1604, when the Emperor Go-Yōzei named the 60-year-old Tokugawa Ieyasu as Shogun. The Tokugawa Shogunate would continue to rule Japan in the emperor's name for another two and a half centuries. But the war that had led to the clash at Sekigahara had created considerable division in Japan, and Ieyasu set about pardoning some of his former enemies and their clans, and stripping the power of others. This included the once all-powerful Toyotomi clan, whose *daimyo* was now

Toyotomi Hideyori, who as an infant had succeeded his father Hideyoshi as clan head in 1599.

Although Ieyasu officially stepped down as Shogun in 1605 in favour of his son Tokugawa Hidetada, the old warlord still retained his old powers, governing the country through his son. However, Ieyasu still had one last problem to deal with. In the aftermath of the Battle of Sekigahara, some of the former leaders of the Western army and the stauncher allies of the Toyotomi clan had switched their allegiance to Toyotomi Hideyori. In effect the young man had become the figurehead of those who opposed the Tokugawa Shogunate, and who saw him as the natural successor to his father, and therefore the rightful ruler of Japan.

Since 1599, Toyotomi Hideyori had lived in his clan's seat at Osaka Castle. In 1611 Tokugawa Ieyasu met the teenage Toyotomi Hideyori, and decided the boy still presented a threat, so he ordered Hideyori and his mother Yodo-dono to leave Osaka, but this didn't result in an end to the growing tension or to the gathering anti-Tokugawa elements in the Toyotomi castle. Attempts to mediate between the two clans proved unsuccessful, and by late 1614 it was clear that Tokugawa Ieyasu had to take action to crush what amounted to a major rebellion. That October the former Shogun gathered an army of 194,000 men and marched on Osaka. As Shogun, his son Hidetada could count on the support of numerous clans and their samurai armies. On 4 December the Shogun's army invested Osaka, and the siege began.

In theory the defenders were commanded by the young Hideyori, but in practice he was just a figurehead, and command was devolved to his gifted general Sanada Yukimura. They had around 100,000 men under their command, protected by wide moats, massive stone walls, well-placed earthen outworks and a complex delta of tributaries of the Tenma River which protected the castle's northern side. On 8 January 1615 the besiegers began bombarding Osaka. After a week of this Yodo-dono offered peace terms, which involved slighting the castle's defences, and promising not to rebel against the Shogun. The Tokugawas agreed, and the winter campaign ended in late January.

By April, though, it was clear that Osaka's defences were still intact and more rebels had gathered there, so the Shogunate army returned and, following minor battles in the surrounding countryside, the siege resumed in June. By then general Sanada Yukimura had been killed and there was no coordinated defence of the castle. With the fall of Osaka inevitable, Hideyori and his mother committed suicide, and the castle fell to the Shogun. Not only did the siege mark the end of the organized resistance against the Tokugawa Shogunate, but it was also the last true clash of the Samurai.

LEFT The defences of Osaka Castle had been augmented by earthworks and ditches. In early January an attack was launched on the castle's Hachomegucho gateway, but thanks to these extra defences this assault by the Shogun's troops was repulsed with heavy losses. (Richard Hook © Osprey Publishing)

LÜTZEN, 16 NOVEMBER 1632

During The Thirty Years War (1618–48) Germany became the battleground of rival armies, fighting over a combination of religious differences and dynastic or imperial dominance. Cities were sacked, the countryside ravaged and the population decimated by war and pestilence. This long-running and destructive war can be divided into different phases, as the campaigns were waged in various parts of Germany, and participating armies joined the fighting or withdrew from it to lick their wounds. A Bohemian phase was followed by campaigning in the Rhineland and Westphalia. When the Danes intervened on the Protestant side the fighting moved to Saxony, but by 1629 the rival armies had all but exhausted themselves, after

just over a decade of war. Still, it was clear that the Holy Roman Emperor Ferdinand II and his military coalition, the Catholic League, was in the ascendancy; therefore, in 1630 Sweden entered the fray to defend German Protestants.

The intervention of the Swedish king Gustavus II Adolphus and his professional army reignited the Protestant cause. Although unable to prevent the Imperialists from sacking the Saxon city of Magdeburg in 1631, Gustavus and his Saxon allies had his revenge on them by destroying their field army that September at the Battle of Breitenfeld. For much of 1632 Gustavus campaigned in the Rhineland and along the Danube, but in September a reinvigorated Imperialist army led by Count Wallenstein returned to Saxony, to threaten the Swedes' lines of supply. Gustavus followed, and in mid-November the two armies met at Lützen, to the south-west of Leipzig. Having just detached a portion of his Imperialist army under General Pappenheim, Wallenstein only had 12,500 men left under his command. He made good use of the terrain, though, deploying his men behind a Lützen to Leipzig road. Gustavus had 18,000 men in his army, most of whom were Swedes.

Mist delayed the start of the battle, but when it cleared mid-morning, Gustavus ordered his two wings of cavalry to charge the waiting enemy. On the Swedish left the ensuing melee was inconclusive but on the right, where Gustavus led the cavalry, he drove back a screen of Imperialist musketeers and horse. When his Swedish infantry joined the fight, the impetus of the Swedish assault threatened to overwhelm Wallenstein's left flank. At that point, however, Pappenheim arrived on the battlefield and launched his own Imperial cavalry into the fray against the Swedish right. In the ensuing clash the losses on both sides were high, but when Pappenheim was mortally wounded by a Swedish roundshot, his men retired and the Imperialist threat evaporated. Both armies were now fully engaged and both were disordered. Gustavus tried to rally in his men, but in the confusion he ran into an Imperialist cavalry unit and was shot dead. Prince Bernhard of Saxe-Weimar assumed command and rallied the disheartened Swedes. He then launched a general advance which pushed the Imperialists back, and overran their guns. Wallenstein's now hopelessly disorganized army began to melt away, and he gave the order to retreat to Leipzig. Both sides had lost 10,000–12,000 men in this bloody battle. Lützen was a hard-won Swedish victory, but the death of Gustavus Adolphus was a major blow to both the Swedish army and the Protestant cause.

LEFT Swedish fortunes at Lützen reached a low point during the early afternoon with the death of the Swedish king, and the subsequent destruction of two brigades of veteran Swedish infantry. The Blue Brigade shown here was all but overrun by Imperialist cuirassiers. (Graham Turner © Osprey Publishing)

MARSTON MOOR, 2 JULY 1644

By the summer of 1644 the English Civil War (1642–46) was almost two years old, and neither the king's armies nor those of parliament had gained the upper hand. The fighting had covered most of England, and although King Charles I had ceased hostilities in Ireland, so he could recall his troops there, the Scottish Covenanters had allied themselves with the Parliamentarians, and had marched south with a sizeable army. While Parliament occupied London, the king had established himself in Oxford, and his forces held large swathes of south-western England and the Midlands. In the north the Marquis of Newcastle's Royalist army had bested his Parliamentarian opponents led by Lord Fairfax. In the spring of 1644, however, the Scots

advancing from the north and the Parliamentarian army of the Eastern Association led by the Earl of Manchester drove the marquis back towards York.

By April York was besieged by three armies: the Scots under the Earl of Leven, Manchester's Eastern Association and Fairfax's resurgent Northern army. In May the king ordered Prince Rupert to march over the Pennines from Lancashire and raise the siege. Rupert marched into Yorkshire and together with the Marquis of Newcastle's Northern Horse he forced the Allies to abandon the siege. Despite the misgivings of the marquis and his advisers, Prince Rupert, who was now in overall command, insisted that the combined Royalist force would now march out from York and give battle.

The Allied army was encamped a few miles to the west on Marston Moor. That morning they had begun marching south, but returned to the moor when they saw Rupert's army approaching. The opposing forces then deployed for battle, with the Allies occupying the high ground between the villages of Tockwith and Long Marston, and the Royalists deploying on the open moor to the north. The Allies had the larger army of around 24,000 men, of which just over half were Scots: 7,000 from the Eastern Association and 4,000 from Lord Fairfax's army. Rupert commanded almost 18,000 men; most from his own army, and the rest from Newcastle's.

The battle opened with a cavalry clash, with Lord Goring's Northern Horse on the Royalist left routing the Fairfax and Scots cavalry ahead of them. On the Parliamentarian left, Manchester's cavalry led by Oliver Cromwell routed their Royalist opponents. While the Royalist victors went on to loot the Allied camp, Cromwell's disciplined cavalry regrouped and fell on the rear of the Royalist army. By then both infantry bodies had clashed, but the outnumbered Royalists were pushed back and then eventually broken. As darkness fell, the last pockets of Royalist resistance were overwhelmed. Around 3,000 Royalists were killed in the battle, and 2,000 Allies. Rupert and the marquis fled the field and, stripped of troops, York would fall two weeks later. This meant the north of England was lost to the Royalists, and Rupert was disgraced, as the king blamed him for the debacle. Marston Moor was decisive and turned the tide of the Civil War.

LEFT After the defeat and rout of the Royalist cavalry, the Parliamentarian infantry pinned the Royalist foot, who were then surrounded by Cromwell's victorious cavalry. Their line of retreat cut off, the Marquis of Newcastle's 'Whitecoats' chose to make a defiant last stand. (Graham Turner © Osprey Publishing)

VIENNA, JULY–SEPTEMBER 1683

Ever since the fall of Constantinople in 1453, the Ottoman Turkish sultans had dreamed of capturing Vienna. It had come close in 1529, in the aftermath of the Ottoman victory over the Hungarians at the Battle of Mohács (1526). Then the Sultan Suleiman I 'the Magnificent' had laid siege to the city with an army of 100,000 men. The siege lasted just two weeks, however, as disease in his camp forced Suleiman to withdraw. Suleiman tried again three years later, but this time his army became bogged down in Hungary. Effectively then, the siege of 1529 represented the high-water mark of the Ottoman invasion of Europe.

After the death of Suleiman in 1566, his successors lacked the enthusiasm for further

campaigns into Hapsburg Europe. It was 1683 before they marched on Vienna again. Then, Sultan Mehmed IV launched a new assault on Vienna, after stirring up a revolt in Hapsburg Hungary. In May his Grand Vizier Kara Mustafa Pasha marched into Hungary at the head of an Ottoman army of 150,000 men.

The Austro-Hungarians fell back towards Vienna, and Mustafa laid siege to the Hapsburg capital on 16 July. The Holy Roman Emperor Leopold I had fled, but the city's garrison commander Count Ernst Rüger von Starhemberg conducted a vigorous defence of the walls. The defenders outnumbered the Ottomans in terms of guns, so the besiegers mined under the walls to avoid counter-battery fire. Meanwhile, word of the siege had reached Rome, and Pope Innocent XI appealed for an international crusade to come to the relief of Vienna. Soon an army of 30,000 troops was assembled under Duke Charles V of Lorraine, made up of contingents from several Germanic states.

In late August it was joined by a Polish force of another 18,000 men, led by King Jan III Sobieski, who assumed overall command of the Christian army. In early September Sobieski and Lorraine advanced on Vienna from the west, through the Wienerwald ('Vienna Woods'), and by 9 September they reached the Kahlberg, a hill overlooking the city. Mustafa redeployed his army to counter this new threat, but continued with the siege. By then the Turks had captured the Burg Revelin on the western side of the city, and their miners were preparing to demolish the city's walls behind it.

On 12 September the battle began with a Turkish assault on the relief force, but this was driven back. Lorraine's German infantry pressed on towards the city, while Sobieski with the cavalry attacked on his right, and carved a path into the heart of the Ottoman army. A final cavalry charge of Polish and German horsemen secured victory and broke the Ottomans' resistance. When Mustafa fled, the rest of his army joined him. The siege was broken, thanks largely to the charge of the Polish winged hussars, who carried all before them. The Ottomans withdrew to the Balkans, and never returned to Vienna. The city – and the Hapsburg Empire – had been saved.

LEFT The siege of Vienna was lifted thanks to a massed assault on the Turkish siege lines by the relief army. The charge was spearheaded by King Jan III Sobieski's Polish winged hussars, who cut a swathe through the defenders which was then exploited by other cavalry. (Peter Dennis © Osprey Publishing)

THE BOYNE, 1 JULY 1690

In the so-called 'Glorious Revolution' of late 1688, the Dutch stadtholder William of Orange seized the English throne in a bloodless military coup, carried out at the behest of English Protestants. King James II of England and VII of Scotland fled to France, and William and his wife Mary, the daughter of the exiled king, were proclaimed joint sovereigns of England and Scotland. France duly declared war, at which point the newly crowned William III assembled 'The Grand Alliance', an anti-French coalition which included the Holy Roman Empire, Spain, the Netherlands, his British kingdoms and several German states. For the most part this coalition's campaigns were fought in Flanders, where English and Scots contingents joined the

Allied armies. However, in the spring of 1689 a 'second front' was opened in Ireland, and the country would soon be plunged into a bloody war whose influence can still be felt today.

At the time, Ireland was held in the name of the Catholic king James by the Earl of Tyrconnel. In March James landed at Kinsale, and after uniting with Tyrconnel, the Jacobite army marched north to besiege the Protestant strongholds of Enniskillen and Londonderry. Both sieges lasted until the summer, but they were eventually lifted when Williamite reinforcements led by the Duke of Schomberg arrived from England. The Jacobites withdrew south to recruit more troops, while the Williamites consolidated their hold in the north. In June William III arrived in Ulster and began his advance south towards Dublin. Half of his polyglot army of 36,000 men were British. The rest of his force was supplied by his European allies, including the Netherlands, Denmark and the French Huguenots.

For his part James commanded around 24,000 men, most of whom were Irish Catholics, supported by a few French regiments. He deployed his army in County Meath to the north of Dublin, behind the River Boyne. As William approached the river, James, fearing he might be outflanked, sent his best French troops upriver to cover a ford. They took no part in the battle, which involved a direct assault across the river by William's men. At the village of Oldbridge, where a ford crossed the river, the Dutch Blue Guards waded over and drove off the Jacobite garrison but were then pinned down by cavalry led by James' illegitimate son, and Schomberg was killed. William then sent his own cavalry across the river. The leading squadrons were bested by the Jacobites, but eventually numbers prevailed, and the Jacobite horse withdrew.

It was now noon. William personally led the next wave across the river at Mill Ford, where a second cavalry clash took place. The Jacobites fought well, but were eventually forced to retire when Williamite infantry arrived to support their horse. With his bridgehead secure, William ordered a general advance up the slope above the river leading to Donore Hill. The Jacobite rearguard contested the advance, and held the hill for a time, but by late afternoon they were forced to withdraw. They marched off in good order, and would continue the campaign for Ireland for another year. After the Boyne, though, Jacobite fortunes faded, and eventually James had to return to exile in France, leaving William firmly on his old throne.

LEFT The Williamite vanguard established a bridgehead on the far bank of the River Boyne, but the Jacobite cavalry then counter-attacked, and threatened to sweep the defenders back into the river. The Duke of Schomberg was attacked and killed during this furious melee. (Graham Turner © Osprey Publishing)

THE AGE OF REASON

BLENHEIM, 13 AUGUST 1704

In late 1700, the death of the childless Spanish king Charles II was followed by a struggle for succession between the French king Louis XIV and the Holy Roman Emperor Leopold I. This led to a war between the two powers which quickly involved much of Europe. The War of the Spanish Succession (1701–14) saw a re-establishment of the anti-French 'Grand Alliance', and in the summer of 1702 an Anglo-Scots army led by the Duke of Marlborough was landed in the Spanish Netherlands (now Belgium), to support the Dutch who were facing a French invasion. Over the next two years the campaign in Flanders expanded to include the Rhineland, and then Bavaria, when the state became a French ally. This posed the risk of a

French drive through Bavaria and Austria to the city of Vienna.

In 1703, the French marshal Villars led an army across the Rhine to join forces with the Bavarians, and campaigned along the Danube, paving the way for this drive into Austria. By early 1704 everything was ready, although Marshal Villars had returned to France, and his army was now commanded by marshals Marsin and Tallard. Marlborough was still in the Spanish Netherlands, as his Dutch allies refused to let their troops leave Flanders. So, Marlborough deceived the Dutch by campaigning in the Moselle, before secretly marching south, his coalition army covering the 250 miles to the Danube in just five weeks. Nobody was more surprised than the two French marshals.

In July Marlborough captured Donauwörth, giving him access to both banks of the Danube, and placing his army between the French and Vienna. Then, in early August, he joined forces with an Imperialist army led by Prince Eugene of Savoy, bringing their total strength up to 56,000 men. This allowed Marlborough to advance on the Franco-Bavarian army which was encamped nearby, and to offer battle. The enemy was encamped to the east, on the north side of the Danube near Höchstädt. The senior French commander, Marshal Tallard, didn't expect an attack, so he was surprised when at dawn reports reached him that the Allies were advancing towards him. He barely had time to deploy his army on the plain behind the Nebel stream before Marlborough's army was upon him.

Marlborough's plan was to storm Blenheim on his left, while Eugene would take the village of Oberglau on his right. That done, the rest of his army would cross the stream and attack the enemy on the open plain between the two villages. In was noon before the attack began, and while the attack on Blenheim was repulsed, Eugene swept the enemy led by Marsin from Oberglau, and sent them retreating in disorder. Having bridged the stream with fascines, Marlborough then unleashed the bulk of his infantry and cavalry across it, and a fierce melee developed. Tallard had already diverted his infantry from the centre to reinforce Blenheim, so when the counter-attacks by the French cavalry failed, his outnumbered infantry were driven from the field. By nightfall Blenheim had surrendered, Tallard was captured and Marlborough's victory was complete. Losses had been high on both sides, but Vienna had been saved, Bavaria effectively knocked out of the war and the French humbled. It was a splendid victory, made all the more remarkable as it was achieved by a polyglot army.

LEFT The initial Allied attack at Blenheim involved the crossing of the Nebel stream while under fire. Then the troops were re-formed before advancing on the French lines. Here, the British Foot Guards are shown crossing the stream, before launching their assault on the French garrison in Blenheim village. (Graham Turner © Osprey Publishing)

FONTENOY, 1745

For much of the 18th century, Europe was riven by a series of dynastic wars, usually fought over the rights of succession among the leading royal houses. The War of the Austrian Succession (1740–48) was one of these, pitching Austria and its 'Pragmatic Allies' (Britain, Hanover and the Netherlands) against a coalition made up of Prussia, France, Spain and Bavaria. Although the fighting spread to North America and India, the real seats of the conflict were in Silesia on the frontier of Prussia and Austria, in Northern Italy and in the 'cockpit of Europe' – the Austrian Netherlands, now Belgium. For the French, the Austrian Netherlands was the key theatre, so after four seasons of largely indecisive campaigning in Flanders, they decided to force

the issue by driving their opponents to fight a decisive battle, on terms favourable to France.

In early 1745 the French commander, Maurice de Saxe, laid siege to Tournai. While capturing this key fortified city would greatly strengthen the French position in Flanders, his main aim was to force the Allied or Pragmatic army commanded by the Duke of Cumberland to attack him, in order to raise the siege. In early May, de Saxe chose a good defensive position near Fontenoy village and deployed his army. On 10 May Allied scouts reconnoitred the French position, and Cumberland decided it was vulnerable to an assault, so he decided to attack the French Army the following morning. Both commanders had approximately 50,000 troops under their command.

The French line was centred on Fontenoy, with its left anchored in woods, and its right on the village of Antoing and the River Schelde. Three redoubts on either side of the village also helped strengthen the French position. On 11 May the battle began with a dawn bombardment and heavy skirmishing in the woods. Then, at 7am, the Dutch infantry attacked the French line between Fontenoy and Antoing. The advance was halted by heavy French fire and was repulsed. Shortly before noon a second Dutch attack was also driven back. Meanwhile, at 11am, Cumberland ordered a massed assault by his British contingent. It advanced towards the French line between Fontenoy and the woods, and despite casualties it succeeded in breaking the French facing them. However, the British advance was halted by repeated charges by the French cavalry, and de Saxe was able to reinforce his line. Gradually the tide of battle turned, as the Allies were now hemmed in by cavalry to their front and infantry on their flanks. Bowing to the inevitable, Cumberland ordered a withdrawal.

At the Battle of Fontenoy the Allies lost up to 10,000 men killed or wounded, while French casualties were marginally lower. But this didn't reflect the moral advantage won by the French. After Fontenoy, de Saxe was lauded as the greatest general of his age and the French Army recovered its military pre-eminence which it had lost after Blenheim. Tournai duly fell to the French, but in 1748, when a peace treaty was signed, the French gave up most of their Flemish territory, thereby squandering the fruits of their costly victory at Fontenoy.

LEFT After the Allied assault was halted to the north of Fontenoy, Marshal de Saxe launched a series of counter-attacks against the Allied infantry. One of these was by the 'Wild Geese', the Irish of Dillon's Regiment, whose costly charge helped demoralize the defenders and force their retreat. (Seán Ó'Brógáin © Osprey Publishing)

ROSSBACH, 5 NOVEMBER 1757

The Seven Years War (1756–63) came about when several European powers formed a coalition to counter the growing power and territorial expansion of Prussia. Chief among these allies were Austria, the Holy Roman Empire, Russia and France. Prussia's only allies were Hanover, a handful of its small German allies and Britain. In the summer of 1756, as the coalition gathered its forces, King Frederick II 'the Great' of Prussia struck first, quickly knocking Saxony out of the coalition then invading the Austrian province of Bohemia. His army met with mixed fortunes, though, and Frederick withdrew into Silesia. The following summer the coalition struck back, as a French army invaded Hanover, defeated the Hanoverians and then advanced westwards

towards Saxony. At the same time the Austrians struck north into Silesia, and it looked like Frederick would be caught between the two coalition armies.

Instead, Frederick left a small blocking force in Saxony, then after regrouping in Berlin he marched into Saxony to confront the French. The French army had been reinforced by Austrian and Imperial contingents, and now numbered over 80,000 men, but it was scattered throughout Saxony and neighbouring Thuringia. The main Franco-Imperialist army of 54,000 men was jointly commanded by Charles, Prince of Soubise, and Prince Joseph of Saxe-Hildburghausen. By late October it was approaching Leipzig where the Prussian army was now concentrating. Then, on 30 October, Frederick learned that Soubise had pulled back behind the River Saale. Frederick immediately ordered his army to advance towards the river. What followed was one of the most masterly military operations of Frederick's career.

On 4 November Frederick's scouts located the enemy encamped a few miles west of the Saale. The French and Imperial allies had concentrated just over 41,000 men, including 10,000 cavalry. That was roughly twice the 22,000-man force available to Frederick, which included 5,000 cavalry. The following morning, Soubise and Hildburghausen grasped the initiative and attempted a march designed to turn the Prussians' left flank. However, this move was spotted by the Prussians and Frederick positioned his small army accordingly. His infantry were deployed in front of their camp between the villages of Bedra and Rossbach. However, Frederick's cavalry under General Seydlitz were deployed to the south-east of the camp, behind Janus Hill, while the bulk of the infantry were covertly moved there too. Effectively, Frederick was planning to ambush his opponents as they approached the hill. As the French and Imperial cavalry climbed its southern slopes Seydlitz unleashed his cavalry, who surprised and routed the enemy horsemen.

Next Frederick moved his hidden infantry forward, screened from their advancing Franco-Imperial counterparts by a fold in the ground to the south-west of the hill. The Allies were still in a long column of march when they ran into the Prussian infantry, who wheeled around the head of the column and blazed away. The fire utterly disordered the French and Imperial foot. When they tried to deploy to meet this threat the Allies were charged in the flank by Seydlitz' cavalry. The whole battle lasted less than 90 minutes and ended with the utter rout of the Allied army. Over 10,000 Franco-Imperial troops were lost in the battle, while Prussian casualties were minimal. The French threat to Prussia had now evaporated, and Frederick was free to deal with the Austrians.

LEFT The French and Imperialist attempt to outflank the Prussians was thwarted by the rapid redeployment of Prussian infantry in their path, buying time for a decisive flanking attack by the Prussian cavalry to develop. Here, Prussian grenadiers are shown firing into the French ranks. (Adam Hook © Osprey Publishing)

LEUTHEN, 6 DECEMBER 1757

After his great victory over the French and Imperialists at Rossbach in early November 1757, the Prussian king Frederick II 'the Great' had successfully thwarted one of the major threats to his kingdom. That summer a Russian army had defeated the small army Frederick had stationed in East Prussia, but the Russians had never capitalized on their victory, so their army was not a direct threat. However, that still left the powerful Austrian army which had invaded the rich Prussian province of Silesia that summer, and was now outside the key fortress city of Breslau. The Austrians had already captured the fortress town of Schweidnitz (now Świdnica). After his victory Frederick reorganized his army at Leipzig, and then began marching them

towards Breslau (now Wrocław). On the way, though, he learned that his small army in Silesia had been defeated outside the city and Breslau had surrendered. The pressure was now on Frederick to turn this grim situation around.

Having completed the 200-mile march in less than two weeks, he reached Parchwitz (now Prochowice), where he absorbed the remnants of the defeated Silesian army into his own force. On 2 December he resumed his advance towards Breslau, now just 30 miles away to the south-east. Two days later he encountered the Austrian army deployed across his path outside the village of Leuthen (now Lutinye), ten miles west of the city. Frederick had 33,000 men under his command, while the Austrian army, commanded by Prince Charles of Lorraine, was twice as large. At dawn on 5 December a freezing fog hid the armies from each other. Frederick turned this to his advantage and, knowing that the Austrians were deployed in front of Leuthen facing east, he led the bulk of his army on a flank march to the south.

The fog hid this manoeuvre until a little after noon, by which time the Prussian army had finished its redeployment and was now facing the southern flank of the Austrian line. Frederick launched the assault at 1pm. The Austrian commander on that flank was General Nadasty, who halted the assault by launching his cavalry in a counter-charge. However, it was defeated by General von Ziethen's Prussian cavalry. He fell back, but a rearguard held the Prussians long enough for a new line to be formed around Leuthen itself. The village was well-defended, but the Prussians eventually broke into it. Leuthen churchyard became a makeshift Austrian redoubt, its defenders repulsing several attacks before the churchyard was finally captured. A desperate Austrian counter-attack on the Prussians massed around the village was launched, but this was eventually driven back by the Prussian cavalry. This brutal cavalry melee was the turning point of the battle. When the Austrian horse retreated, the rest of their army wavered, and as darkness fell the Austrians were in full retreat. It had been a bloody battle, with over 6,000 Prussians and 10,000 Austrians killed or wounded. Another 12,000 Austrians were captured, and the remnants of the vanquished army withdrew back into Bohemia. For Frederick the Great it was a spectacular victory, and today Leuthen is regarded as his finest battle.

LEFT Frederick's flanking attack at Leuthen took the Austrians by surprise. The assault by his leading regiments drove in the Austrian left wing, and pushed them back in disorder as far as Leuthen village. Here, a Württemberg regiment's attempt wavers in the face of the steady Prussian advance. (Adam Hook © Osprey Publishing)

TICONDEROGA, 8 JULY 1758

While the Seven Years War (1756–63) was primarily fought in Europe, the conflict had begun in North America two years earlier, as clashes erupted along the frontier between the British and French colonies. Here, the ensuing struggle is generally known as 'The French and Indian War'. As tensions mounted, the French began work on Fort Carillon at Ticonderoga on the shores of Lake Champlain. It was designed to prevent a British invasion northwards into New France (now Canada). The fighting remained relatively low key until the summer of 1756, when the Marquis of Montcalm arrived to command the French forces in the province. Over the next year he led two attacks on British territory, capturing Fort Oswego in 1756 and

Fort William-Henry the following year. So far, the French had enjoyed the upper hand on the frontier, but during the winter of 1757–58 the British sent reinforcements to North America, and plans were laid for a full-scale invasion of New France the following spring.

By early summer a British army of 16,000 men under General James Abercrombie was gathered at the southern end of Lake George. Some 6,000 of these were British regulars, and the rest American provincial militia and rangers. On 5 July these were moved by boat to the northern end of the lake, where the following morning they were safely disembarked. Abercrombie was now less than four miles from Ticonderoga. After an initial skirmish the British advance was unopposed, and on 7 July Abercrombie's troops reached Ticonderoga.

It was now clear the French had strengthened Fort Carillon's defences, as Montcalm had built earthworks on Ticonderoga Heights, between the British and the fort itself, the earth and log defences strengthened by an abatis of felled trees. The position was defended by around 3,000 French regulars. Abercrombie decided to attack the following day with 3,600 men, a mixture of British regulars and American provincial militia.

This battle began soon after 12.30pm, when New York militia on the British left advanced to within range of the earthworks. This, though, was premature, as Abercrombie hadn't yet ordered an attack. Reinforcements were then sent forward to support the New Yorkers. This meant that the assault was uncoordinated. The French regulars held their ground, however, and inflicted heavy casualties on the attackers, who were unable to reach the earthworks. Abercrombie tried to regroup his forces, but most of his units kept fighting through the afternoon. The closest the British came to a breakthrough was at 5pm, when the 42nd ('Black Watch') Highlanders assaulted the north side of the entrenchments. Some even reached the earthworks before being cut down; the regiment lost half its men that day. By 7pm it was clear that the assault on Ticonderoga had failed, and the British withdrew to their boats. In all they lost around 2,500 men, killed, wounded or missing, while French losses were considerably lower. It was the bloodiest battle of the war in the Americas, and ensured that New France would survive for another year, until Montcalm's death at the Battle of Quebec.

LEFT Throughout the afternoon, waves of poorly coordinated assaults were launched on the French defences, but all attempts to find a weak spot were unsuccessful. Instead, the attackers, including the 42nd Foot ('the Black Watch'), pictured here, were driven back with extremely heavy casualties. (Patrice Courcelle © Osprey Publishing)

QUEBEC (THE PLAINS OF ABRAHAM), 13 SEPTEMBER 1759

After their repulse at Ticonderoga in 1758 the British realized that New France could only be conquered by deploying overwhelming force. Their cause was helped in late July 1758 when the Fortress of Louisbourg fell to the British. This French fortress guarded the seaward approaches to the St. Lawrence River, which meant the British could now attack Quebec, the heart of the French colony. This attack would be carried out in the summer of 1759 by Major-General James Wolfe, who had distinguished himself at Louisbourg. Simultaneously a drive

on Lake Champlain would be made in sufficient numbers to guarantee the capture of Fort Carillon. Sure enough, that summer the French abandoned the fort as General Jeffery Amherst's large British army advanced northwards, and by the end of the summer it had reached the southern side of the upper St. Lawrence River.

Meanwhile, on 28 June Wolfe's army of 7,000 was landed three miles below Quebec. The city's defences appeared formidable, but morale among Montcalm's 3,500-strong garrison was low. Wolfe's initial attempt to establish a bridgehead on the north side of the St. Lawrence was thwarted on 31 June, so, while his men besieged the city, he laid plans for another assault. On the night of 12/13 September Wolfe's men were transported by boat to land at l'Anse-au-Foulon, a short distance upriver from Quebec, at the foot of a steep bluff. Preceded by the light infantry the army scrambled up the slope, to emerge onto the Plains of Abraham, a large open space to the west of Quebec. By 8am Wolfe's small army was deployed into line, where it faced the similarly arrayed French, who had marched out of Quebec to meet them.

The battle that followed lasted less than half an hour. The British line formed a horseshoe-shaped formation, with both flanks folded back, to protect them from the numerous French skirmishers. In the centre, five regular French battalions and two more of Canadian militia formed a single line of 1,950 men, while across a cornfield, Wolfe's centre of 1,500 men was made up of six regular battalions. Montcalm also had 1,500 militiamen and Indian units acting as skirmishers, while Wolfe had another 1,000 men on his flanks, along with his sole reserve, the 48th Foot. At around 10am Montcalm decided to force the issue with a rapid advance. The attack was ragged as the militiamen stopped to fire, then held back. The British held their fire until the French were 30 yards away, and then fired a devastating volley. This stopped the French cold, and after a second massed British volley they broke and ran. Wolfe, though, had already been mortally wounded, probably by shots from French skirmishers, and he died at the moment of victory, as his men pursued the French into Quebec. Montcalm was also hit during the retreat, and died a few hours later. His army lost around 1,500 dead and wounded that day, roughly twice the British casualties. More importantly, the French had also lost Canada. With Quebec in British hands the colony was no longer defensible, and it would be surrendered the following year.

LEFT In what later became known as 'The Battle on the Plains' the outcome was decided in a matter of minutes after the two lines of infantry began firing at a range of just 30 yards. In the centre the British 43rd and 47th Foot fired double-shotted volleys, which broke the French with one volley. (Gerry Embleton © Osprey Publishing)

SARATOGA, 19 SEPTEMBER–7 OCTOBER 1777

The American War of Independence pitted a small but professional British army against a much larger Continental army of raw militiamen and self-taught regular soldiers. It was also fought over a vast area, much of which was little more than wilderness. Any significant loss of British troops would have a major impact on the course of the war. By the spring of 1777 the conflict was over two years old and, despite several British successes, neither side had gained the upper hand.

British strategists developed a bold plan to cut the American colonies in two, along the line of the Hudson River, to the north of New York. What looked good on a map, though, wasn't necessarily so practical in the American

backwoods. The plan required Lieutenant-General 'Gentleman Johnny' Burgoyne to advance south from Canada, while General William Howe marched north from New York. The two armies would meet at Albany, in upper New York State. At first Burgoyne's northern force did well. His small army of 7,200 British and Hessian regulars marched down Lake Champlain to capture Fort Ticonderoga, then advanced south into the Hudson Valley. Howe, though, had reneged on his part of the plan and had taken his army south to Philadelphia instead, so Burgoyne was on his own.

In mid-September Burgoyne's scouts came upon an American army blocking his advance from Saratoga to Albany. General Horatio Gates' 7,000 men were entrenched in a strong position on Bemis Heights. On 19 September, as Burgoyne's army approached the heights, the 3,000-strong left flank American division under General Benedict Arnold advanced to harry the British as they advanced. The two forces clashed around Freeman's Farm. The battle fought around the farm and surrounding woods was indecisive, despite Gates reinforcing Arnold, and Burgoyne calling up his reserves. The battle ended when darkness fell, with the British losing around 600 men killed or wounded, and the Americans half that. An impasse followed as Burgoyne pondered how to force his way through the American position. His main hope was that General Henry Clinton would advance from New York, but this never occurred.

Meanwhile, animosity between Gates and Arnold grew, and Arnold was replaced. With his supplies dwindling, Burgoyne decided to risk everything on one last assault. On 7 October he ordered a reconnaissance in force of Bemis Heights, but his men ran into the American army advancing towards them. They were driven back to Burgoyne's line of redoubts, which were then assaulted by the Americans. Gates had 11,000 men now, while Burgoyne's force had been reduced to half that. Surprisingly the American assault was led by Arnold, who had defied Gates to join the attack. While he overran the British right flank, Burgoyne's main line held firm and by nightfall the Americans were repulsed. Burgoyne's position was untenable, though, and he withdrew to Saratoga where his army was surrounded. It surrendered on 17 October. The battles at Saratoga might have been small but they decided the fate of a continent. The American victory inspired the French to join the fight on the American side, and while the war dragged on, it was now almost impossible for Britain to win the struggle.

LEFT The height of the second battle came after the British were driven back to their starting positions. These were anchored by two redoubts, one of which was stormed by General Benedict Arnold and his men. Arnold was wounded, though, just before the defending Hessian grenadiers were driven off. (Adam Hook © Osprey Publishing)

YORKTOWN, SEPTEMBER–OCTOBER 1781

In the three years following the American victory at Saratoga the fortunes of war had ebbed and flowed across the 13 colonies. General Howe captured Washington but was unable to hold the American capital, and led a fighting retreat back to New York. Then in late 1779, his replacement General Clinton landed a large British force at Charleston. The Carolinas had been riven by a bitterly fought civil war between Loyalists and Patriots, and Clinton planned to draw on this strong Loyalist support to secure the region for the British crown. After capturing Charleston he handed his army over to Charles, Lord Cornwallis, who went on to win a string of victories over the Americans commanded by General Gates. American resistance stiffened,

though, when Gates was succeeded by General Nathanael Greene. While Cornwallis' small army defeated Greene at the Battle of Guilford Courthouse in March 1781, his army was so battered that he had to abandon the Carolinas and withdraw into Virginia.

British troops led by the newly defected General Arnold had secured a foothold in Virginia, and in May Cornwallis joined him. Meanwhile a Franco-American force of 3,550 men led by the French Marquis de Lafayette arrived in Virginia, and the two armies manoeuvred and skirmished until August when Cornwallis withdrew to Yorktown on the York River, where he could maintain sea communications with Clinton in New York. That prompted the American commander General George Washington to march south with the Continental Army, accompanied by a French force led by the Comte de Rochambeau. In late August a French fleet arrived to help blockade Cornwallis, then in early September a British fleet led by Admiral Thomas Graves engaged it in the Battle of the Capes, but was driven off and had to withdraw to New York. That meant that Cornwallis and his 8,000 men were trapped.

LEFT When General Cornwallis' small British army was besieged in Yorktown, earthworks were built to augment the town's defences. Two advanced redoubts hindered Franco-American attempts to invest the town, and so these were stormed and taken in a bitterly contested night assault. (Graham Turner © Osprey Publishing)

Washington arrived on 28 September and laid siege to Yorktown. He had 9,500 American and 7,800 French troops under his command, supported by a powerful artillery train. Cornwallis was forced to abandon his outer defences, and the bombardment of the small port's inner defences began on 9 October. Some six days later two key redoubts, No. 9 and No. 10, were taken by Franco-American storming parties in a night attack. This allowed Washington to move his trenches and parallels closer to the British earthworks, and the bombardment continued. Cornwallis' situation was becoming desperate. Still, he had one last roll of the dice. In the early morning of 16 October the British attacked the besieger's earthworks. Although six guns were put out of action, the small assaulting force was driven back into Yorktown.

The end was now inevitable. The following day Cornwallis opened negotiations with Washington, and on 19 October his battered army marched out of Yorktown and surrendered. A week too late, General Clinton reached Virginia waters with 7,000 men, but on learning of the capitulation his force sailed back to New York. The Franco-American victory at Yorktown meant that to all intents and purposes the Americans had won their independence, and a peace was finally signed in November 1782. The British had lost their American colonies, and the United States had emerged onto the world stage.

THE NAPOLEONIC ERA

TOULON, AUGUST–DECEMBER 1793

When the French Revolution erupted in May 1789, France was pitched into a period of immense social and political upheaval. By 1792 the monarchical powers intervened in an attempt to end the Revolution. Instead, Europe became embroiled in the decade-long French Revolutionary Wars (1792–1802). The establishment of a French Republic in September 1792 was followed by 'The Terror', where public executions became the norm as the Republicans sought to cleanse France of all traces of the *ancien régime*. Outrage following the execution of the French king Louis XVI in January 1793 led to an escalation of the conflict as Britain and Spain joined the anti-French coalition. On land the zeal of the French Revolutionary armies

overcame their lack of discipline and training, and after repelling an invasion at the Battle of Valmy in 1792, the raw French armies held their own the following year in the bitter campaigns fought in the Spanish Netherlands.

In the French Navy, though, the Revolution led to a lack of serviceable ships and the trained crew to man them. 'The Terror' had also led to a cull among the navy's officers, which limited the fleet's ability to operate effectively. By contrast Britain's Royal Navy had been expanded, and now powerful fleets blockaded the French naval bases at Brest and Toulon. Then, in the summer of 1793, French Royalists seized control of Toulon, and evicted the port's Republicans. They then requested help from the British Mediterranean Fleet, which was commanded by Admiral Sir Samuel Hood. Thus, on 28 August, a coalition force of 13,000 British, Spanish, Piedmontese and Neapolitan troops arrived to help defend this key port – home to a third of France's navy. By securing these ships, Hood had ensured Britain's complete naval mastery of the Mediterranean. Holding Toulon, however, would be a much greater challenge.

On 8 September a French army of 12,000 men arrived and laid siege to the port. Their commander, General Jean Carteaux, a former artist, had no knowledge of siegecraft, and as his artillery commander had been wounded, he relied on a 24-year-old Corsican-born captain to take over. He was Napoleon Bonaparte. He transformed the siege, gathering guns and men from nearby depots, and although he also had no combat experience, he was able to develop a plan to drive the Allies from the port. He recognized that one particular defensive bastion, Fort Musgrave, was the key to Toulon. From its ramparts, which overlooked the harbour, he could bombard both the town and the Allied fleet. But indecision delayed the taking of the fort. In November Carteaux was replaced by the ineffective General François Doppet, followed by the far more able General Jacques Dugommier.

Dugommier immediately saw the merits of Bonaparte's plan, and early on 16 December, after a preliminary bombardment, the fort was stormed and taken. As Bonaparte predicted, this made the port untenable for the allies. Orders were given to evacuate Toulon, but panic among the Allied defenders led to a rapid collapse of the port's landward defences, so Hood ordered an immediate evacuation. However, the last-minute destruction of the French fleet was mishandled, and over half was left to be recaptured by the French. Afterwards, the Republicans executed the Royalist insurgents of Toulon, while Bonaparte, the man who had ensured the recapture of the port, would soon be destined for greater things.

LEFT The young Napoleon Bonaparte grasped that the key to the recapture of Toulon was possession of the hills overlooking the harbour. He established several hilltop batteries like the one shown here, and then planned to assault and capture the enemy-held forts guarding the remaining heights. (Adam Hook © Osprey Publishing)

THE NILE, 1 AUGUST 1798

By 1798 the French had defeated the combined armies of Europe and were now considering an amphibious attack on Britain. However, France's most successful general Napoleon Bonaparte proposed a much more ambitious venture. By attacking Egypt, he could threaten British control of India, and extend France's influence throughout the Middle East. The ruling Directoire approved this wild scheme, and the Army of the Orient was gathered in Toulon. In June 1798 it slipped out to sea during a storm and headed to Malta, which was duly captured. From there the fleet of warships and transports headed east up the Mediterranean and made landfall in Alexandria on 29 June. Meanwhile, Lord St. Vincent, commanding the British

Mediterranean Fleet, sent a strong detachment off in pursuit. It was commanded by Rear Admiral Horatio Nelson.

The two fleets narrowly missed each other at sea and again off Egypt. However, on 1 August Nelson's scouts sighted French transports off Alexandria, and a few hours later the main French fleet was spotted a few miles to the east in Aboukir Bay. The fleet's commander, Vice Admiral Brueys, had anchored his 14 ships-of-the-line parallel to the coast, with his four frigates and squadron of gunboats closer inshore, under the guns of Aboukir Castle. His 120-gun flagship *L'Orient* lay at the centre of the long French line. It was dusk when the British approached, and Brueys expected the British to lie off and attack the following morning, so his fleet went 'to quarters', but remained at anchor. Nelson, though, approaching in line from seaward, signalled his captains to prepare for battle. At 6.30pm, as night fell, Nelson's similarly sized fleet swept into the bay, aiming for the head of the French line.

Although the ship-of-the-line *Culloden* ran aground on shoals, the rest continued on, under fire from the starboard batteries of the anchored French ships. As the leading ship *Goliath* passed the bow of the leading French ship *Guerrier* the crew raked her, then swung around *Guerrier's* port side to pass down the unengaged port side of the French line at point-blank range. Others followed, and these teamed up with the rearmost British ships, who ranged themselves along the starboard side of the French ships. The two rows of British ships worked their way down the French line, firing into the ships from both sides at once. The French fought with great bravery, but there was little they could do. One after the other the leading French ships were battered into submission and struck their colours.

Eventually it was the turn of Bruey's *L'Orient* which dismasted the smaller *Bellerophon*, but the French flagship was outnumbered and surrounded. Finally, at 10.30pm, as fires reached the ship's magazine, *Bellerophon* blew up in an immense explosion. With that the three rearmost French ships led by Rear Admiral Villeneuve cut their anchor cables and fled. Seven years later, Villeneuve would face Nelson again at Trafalgar. That night, though, ten French ships-of-the-line had been captured and one destroyed. Nelson's victory was complete, and Bonaparte's army was now stranded in Egypt. Without setting foot ashore, Nelson had utterly confounded Bonaparte's great venture.

LEFT During the British fleet's approach to the French fleet anchored in Aboukir Bay, Nelson's ships were exposed to the broadsides of the French van. Nelson, though, was confident that his own daring plan, to close on the enemy from two sides at once, would lead to the annihilation of the French fleet. (Peter Dennis © Osprey Publishing)

MARENGO, 14 JUNE 1800

In August 1799, General Bonaparte turned over command of his Army of Egypt and returned to France with his staff. His soldiers were left behind, and surrendered in early 1801. By then, however, Bonaparte had gone on to greater things. On his return he found the unpopular Directoire was in turmoil, and opponents to it invited the much-fêted general to become their military ally. With Bonaparte's help the plotters swept to power in a coup and governed France as a three-man consulate. Bonaparte's reward for his support was to be named First Consul. In effect he was now a military dictator, but his primary task was to deal with the new anti-French military coalition which had been formed while he was in Egypt. At the time, French

armies were active in the Low Countries, on the Rhine and in Italy, but it was this last theatre that was proving the most problematic.

The Russians and Austrians had ejected the French from Italy; therefore, Bonaparte's job was to restore French control of the region which he had so masterfully conquered before his Egyptian venture. In May, Bonaparte led an army of 51,000 men across the Alps to emerge in the north Italian plains behind the main Austrian army of General Michael von Melas. The Austrian general was effectively cut off, and so had to either sidestep Bonaparte or fight him. By 13 June the two armies came into contact with each other on the flat plains near Alessandria in the Piedmont. Early the following morning, several columns of Austrian troops crossed the small River Bormida to attack the isolated French division on its eastern bank. Bonaparte had 28,000 men on the field but they were scattered over a wide area. This meant Melas had a chance to defeat the French Army in detail.

At 10am General Andreas O' Reilly's Austrian column clashed with General Victor's smaller French division near Marengo, but desperate charges by supporting French cavalry slowed the Austrian assault. However, as more Austrian columns joined the battle the French were pushed back. Bonaparte still thought this Austrian attack was a diversion, so he refused to commit his reserves. However, General Jean Lannes averted an immediate disaster by committing his own division, but he soon came under increasing pressure from the more numerous Austrians. The French had now been driven back three miles but at noon Bonaparte realized Victor and Lannes were facing all of Melas' army.

Consequently, he ordered his scattered army to concentrate and threw reinforcements into the fight as soon as they arrived. By 2pm a French defeat seemed certain, but the divisions of generals Desaix and Boudet arrived from the south and turned the tide of the battle. Although Desaix was killed in this counter-attack, his men halted the Austrian advance, then a cavalry charge by General Kellerman's Cavalry Corps sent the Austrian line reeling back. By late afternoon the Austrians were in full retreat. Bonaparte's victory at Marengo secured Italy for the French and forced the Austrians to sue for peace. It also boosted Bonaparte's reputation and allowed him to consolidate his grip on power within France.

LEFT The ferocity of the Austrian assaults at Marengo took Bonaparte by surprise, and his French troops were extremely hard-pressed. The nadir came when Bonaparte committed his Consular Guard to stem the tide, and it was routed. The day was saved, though, by the arrival of French reinforcements. (Christa Hook © Osprey Publishing)

TRAFALGAR, 21 OCTOBER 1805

The Treaty of Amiens in October 1802 brought an uneasy peace to Europe but it was clear this wouldn't last. Sure enough, hostilities resumed between Britain and France in May 1803, and a French invasion fleet gathered in the Channel ports. This amphibious assault never materialized, however, largely due to the vigilance of the Royal Navy. In December 1804 Spain entered the war on France's side, coinciding with the elevation of Consul for Life Bonaparte to Emperor Napoleon I of France. This meant that now the Spanish fleet of 29 ships-of-the-line was placed at Napoleon's disposal. In March 1805, Vice Admiral Villeneuve slipped out of Toulon with 11 ships-of-the-line, evading Vice Admiral Nelson's blockading squadron to reach the

Atlantic, picking up six Spanish ships-of-the-line as he passed Cadiz. In May he took his Allied fleet to the West Indies, then returned to Europe, reaching the Bay of Biscay by late July.

After a brush with a British fleet off Cape Finisterre, Villeneuve realized that he wouldn't be able to link up with the main French fleet in Brest, so he headed south to Cadiz. Nelson had pursued Villeneuve to the West Indies and back, and now lay off Cadiz waiting for Villeneuve to come out. Sure enough, in September Napoleon ordered Villeneuve to return to the Mediterranean, so on 19–20 October the Allied fleet left Cadiz and set a course towards Gibraltar. At dawn on 21 October, some 15 miles off Cape Trafalgar, Nelson's fleet was sighted to the west. Villeneuve turned his fleet about and made for the safety of Cadiz, 25 miles to the north. It was too late, though, as despite the light winds battle was now inevitable. Nelson deployed his 27 ships-of-the-line into two columns, one led by himself in his flagship *Victory*, and the other led by Vice Admiral Collingwood in *Royal Sovereign*.

Villeneuve's fleet consisted of 33 ships-of-the-line; 18 French commanded by Villeneuve himself, flying his flag in *Bucentaure*, and 15 Spanish ones led by Admiral Federico Gravina.

The Allied squadrons were intermingled, and continued on to the north as Nelson's columns sailed east, heading towards the enemy at right angles to it. The Allies opened fire at 11.35pm, but the British didn't reply, as their broadside guns didn't bear on the enemy ships. The leading British ships suffered, but they remained on course, and at 12.15pm they cut the Allied line in two places. The battle now dissolved into a short-range melee, with the British massing their ships against the central and southern portions of the enemy line. Shortly after 1.15pm a French sharpshooter on *Redoutable* shot Nelson, and he was carried below.

The fight continued, however, as the better-trained British crews battered the Allied ships into submission. They began to strike, and when the unengaged Allied vanguard sailed off towards Cadiz, they were left to their fate. Shortly before Nelson died at 4.30pm, he was told he had won a stunning victory, capturing or destroying 18 enemy ships-of-the-line. Four more would be added to the tally later. The death of the brilliant Nelson was a grievously bitter blow, but his last battle had achieved the total annihilation of the enemy fleet, safeguarded Britain from invasion, and guaranteed British naval supremacy for the remainder of the war.

LEFT Nelson's unconventional tactics at Trafalgar resulted in the breaking of the Anglo-French line in two places. While this involved a lengthy approach that exposed his flagship *Victory* and her consorts to a heavy fire, when they broke the line they could fire into the enemy ships at point-blank range. (Peter Dennis © Osprey Publishing)

AUSTERLITZ, 2 DECEMBER 1805

In early 1805 the Third Coalition was formed against France, as Britain was joined by Austria, Russia and Sweden. The new allies devised an ambitious scheme, involving operations in Italy and Bavaria, as well as the Baltic coast, which would culminate in an invasion of France by a combined Austro-Russian army. Faced with this threat, Napoleon abandoned his plans to invade Britain. Instead, his newly reorganized Grande Armée would strike the Austrians before the Russians could march west to join them. By late September seven French corps, a Bavarian one and the Imperial Guard were massed along the Rhine. In all, Napoleon had 210,000 men at his command. A rapid advance to the east saw the French reach the Danube to the east of General

Mack's Austrian army of 72,000 men which was concentrated around Ulm. After two weeks of manoeuvre, Mack surrendered his army with hardly a shot being fired.

Napoleon then struck eastwards towards Vienna, which was captured on 12 November. The remains of the Austrian army had retreated to the north-east, and at Olmütz joined forces with 55,000 Russians under General Kutuzov, accompanied by Tsar Alexander I. The Austrians, accompanied by the Emperor Francis I, brought the Allied army's strength up to 86,000 men. The combined army then marched south to find Napoleon. Meanwhile, the French emperor had marched north from Vienna to Brünn, 60 miles to the north. Having left troops behind to guard Vienna and his lines of communication, Napoleon had just under 70,000 men under his command. He realized he had to defeat his foes, to break the enemy coalition. He selected what he saw as the perfect battleground, 14 miles east of Brünn near the village of Austerlitz, and to lure in his opponents he even let them occupy the high ground of the Pratzen Heights.

At dawn on 2 December the Allied army stood on the heights in three large columns. Tsar Alexander demanded they attack that morning, in case Napoleon withdrew, so three Allied columns on the left advanced on Marshal Soult's French corps, deployed to the west of them, while another Russian column attacked Marshal Lannes' corps, on Soult's left flank. Napoleon, though, kept the bulk of his army hidden. Soult bore the brunt of the Allied attack, but Marshal Davout's small corps, which had been held in reserve, marched to his aid, and the line held. By now the Pratzen Heights were only lightly held, so at 8.30am, as 'the sun of Austerlitz' shone, Napoleon ordered Soult's unengaged left flank to advance, supported by Marshal Bernadotte's corps, the French cavalry and the Imperial Guard.

The heights were taken, and the French held on to them in the face of several counter-attacks, then Bernadotte turned south to trap the bulk of the Allied army that was still fighting Soult. It quickly broke and ran, fleeing across frozen lakes to escape the French. By 4pm the battle was over. The French had lost 9,000 men killed or wounded in the battle, but the Allied casualty list was much higher: 16,000 casualties, and 11,000 more captured. While Russia would fight on, Austria immediately agreed to a humiliating peace. Arguably, Austerlitz was Napoleon's greatest victory – and his most complete.

LEFT When the French seized the summit of the Pratzen Heights the Allies realized they had lost the key position on the battlefield, so the Russian Guard were ordered to retake the heights. The Guard cavalry caused havoc, and even captured a French eagle, but the French grimly held their ground. (Christa Hook © Osprey Publishing)

WAGRAM, 5–6 JULY 1809

In the years following his victory at Austerlitz, Napoleon went on to defeat the Prussians at Jena–Auerstadt in October 1806, and the Russians at Eylau the following February. The Prussians made peace, and when the Russians were defeated again at Friedland in June 1807, Tsar Alexander too signed a peace treaty with France. Napoleon now dominated continental Europe although France's increasingly bloody involvement in Spain raised the prospect of a revival of opposition in Central Europe while Napoleon was distracted. When Prussia and Russia refused to fight, Austria decided to go to war on its own, so in early April 1809 an Austrian army invaded Bavaria and Central Europe was plunged into a new war.

Archduke Charles commanding the Austrian army hoped to seize Bavaria before the French could react. Napoleon and his Grande Armée marched there quickly and Charles was defeated at Abensberg and Eckmühl, and forced to withdraw. Charles retired towards Vienna, pursued by Napoleon, and the Austrian capital fell on 14 May. By then Charles had abandoned the city and withdrawn to the northern bank of the Danube, a few miles to the north-east. Napoleon needed a decisive victory over the Austrians, so his engineers bridged the river and the French established a bridgehead on the north bank. But on 21 May, Charles counter-attacked. In the two-day Battle of Aspern-Essling that followed, the Austrians launched repeated assaults which almost overwhelmed the bridgehead, eventually forcing the French to withdraw to Lobau, an island in the Danube. Napoleon had suffered his first major defeat.

As his battered army recovered on Lobau, Napoleon planned his revenge. He now had 188,000 men in seven corps, plus the Imperial Guard, while Charles commanded 155,000 in seven corps. On the night of 4–5 July Napoleon moved his army onto the north bank of the river,

then, after some brisk fighting, he deployed on the plain to the north. Both sides planned to renew the fight the following morning. At dawn on 6 July the Austrians attacked first, driving back the Saxons of Bernadotte's IX Corps on the French left wing. The French line was eventually stabilized by the arrival of Marshal Masséna's IV Corps. Masséna then counter-attacked against the Austrian right, while Marshal Oudinot's II Corps and Marshal Davout's III Corps pinned the Austrian left and centre, their line supported by a massed battery of over 100 guns.

At 2pm Napoleon realized the Austrian centre near the village of Wagram had been weakened, so he attacked there with two Italian corps led by Marshal Macdonald, whose men were formed into one giant column. The Austrian centre collapsed under the weight of this assault, and Charles' army was split in two. By late afternoon the two Austrian wings were in retreat, leaving the field to the French. The battle had been won, but it was Napoleon's bloodiest victory yet. His army lost 40,000 men that day, as did the Austrians. Still, the Austrians quickly sued for peace and, apart from Spain, peace was restored in Napoleon's empire.

LEFT At Wagram the initial French assault by Marshal Masséna drove these Austrians of General Klenau's Corps from the fortified villages of Aspern and Essling. That then gave Napoleon the room he needed to deploy his Grande Armée in the vast plain beyond, before advancing on the main Austrian position. (Jeffrey Burn © Osprey Publishing)

SALAMANCA, 22 JULY 1812

Spain had been a half-hearted ally of the French, while Portugal was a British ally, so in March 1808 Napoleon marched a small army across Spain to subdue Portugal. He also orchestrated a regime change in Spain, replacing the monarch with his brother Joseph Bonaparte. In May the Spanish people rose in armed revolt, and the French became embroiled in a bitter war where atrocity became commonplace. The 'Spanish Ulcer' drained the French Army of men and resources, as Spanish guerrillas preyed on French garrisons, patrols and lines of communication. The Spanish regular army's contribution was less effective, but in August 1808 a small British army under Sir Arthur Wellesley landed in Portugal and defeated the French. He was recalled home,

though, and his successor Sir John Moore was killed at Corunna the following January.

Wellesley, who later became the Duke of Wellington, returned to Portugal the following spring and secured his hold on Lisbon. Napoleon's leading marshals' attempts to drive him from Portugal were thwarted by Allied victories at Talavera, Buçaco, Fuentes de Oroño and Albuera, achieved by Wellington with military support from the Portuguese and Spanish. In early 1812 Wellington's capture of the frontier fortresses of Badajoz and Ciudad Rodrigo secured Portugal, and allowed him to venture into Spain itself. He was helped, though, by the fact that Napoleon was fully occupied with the invasion of Russia. That summer Wellington's Anglo-Portuguese army advanced into Spain, pursuing Marshal Marmont's French army as it withdrew from Portugal. In late July he caught up with it near the city of Salamanca in Castile and Léon. They were well-matched in numbers; Wellington had 52,000 men and Marmont 49,000 men.

Wellington occupied the better position; therefore, Marmont attempted to outflank him to the west. The French Army became dangerously strung out on the march, however, and so at 3pm Wellington launched a devastating attack by General Packenham's division against the rear of the French columns. Marmont turned his army to face his assailants but was badly wounded, depriving his army of leadership when it was dearly needed. Soon the French left wing had been put to flight. The French were then hit by an equally effective assault by General Leith's division against their centre, near the village of Los Arapiles. By 4.30pm four French divisions had been broken.

However, to the east General Cole's division attacked the French-held hill known as the Greater Arapiles. It was repulsed with heavy losses. The senior French commander there, General Clausel, then ordered a counter-attack by whatever troops he could gather. His attack drove Cole's battered division back, but it ran into Wellington's reserve which had been deployed in its path. Here, the Anglo-Portuguese musketry proved devastating, and Clausel's men were forced to retreat. At 6pm Wellington ordered Clinton's largely unengaged division to take the Greater Arapiles, which they did, but only after suffering heavy casualties from General Ferrey's division. By evening the French were in full retreat, but Wellington's army was too exhausted to pursue. His Anglo-Portuguese force had lost 5,200 men that day, but Marmont's losses were much greater, around 14,000 men. Salamanca was a major blow to the French and the turning point of the Peninsular War. In August, Wellington's army was able to liberate Madrid, proving that France's grip on Spain had been fatally weakened.

LEFT At Salamanca Wellington's devastatingly effective assault on the left and centre French line broke the three French divisions deployed there. The men of Leith's division, who assaulted General Macune's French Division, even managed to capture the eagle of the 62nd Regiment de Ligne. (Bill Younghusband © Osprey Publishing)

BORODINO, 7 SEPTEMBER 1812

In June 1812, Napoleon invaded Russia at the head of 430,000 men. His Grande Armée had been reinforced by numerous allied contingents, from Germany, Italy, Poland and elsewhere. For the most part the Russians retreated in the face of Napoleon's advancing troops, but unsuccessful stands were made at Mogilev and Smolensk. This 'Fabian tactic' preserved the Russian army as it drew back towards Moscow, but it proved highly unpopular, and in August Tsar Alexander appointed General Mikhail Kutuzov as the commander-in-chief of the Russian army. Patriotic fervour in Russia necessitated that a defensive battle be fought before the invaders reached Moscow. Kutuzov selected Borodino, 70 miles west of Moscow, as

the place to make his stand. During late August the position there was strengthened by redoubts and earthworks, then Kutuzov deployed his army and waited for Napoleon.

On 5 September the French advance guard clashed with the Russians as the Grande Armée approached Borodino. Kutuzov had 106,000 men under his command, made up of General Barclay de Tolly's First Army, Prince Bagration's Second Army and the Russian Guard. This force included 24,000 regular cavalry and Cossacks, and 10,000 poorly equipped militia. Kutuzov also had 640 guns, some of which were deployed in his earthworks. Campaign losses and the need to protect flanks and the lines of communication had reduced Napoleon's Grande Armée to 135,000 men, including the Imperial Guard. This force included 28,000 cavalry, as well as 580 guns. Napoleon's unsubtle battle plan centred around a massed frontal assault, while diversionary attacks were launched at the Russian flanks.

The battle began soon after dawn on 7 September. On the French left, Prince Eugene's largely Italian corps attacked the Russian right wing, while Prince Poniatowski's Polish corps assaulted the Russian left wing, then Marshal Davout launched the main assault against the Russian centre. After some hard fighting he threw the defenders out of the flèches – small arrowhead-shaped earthworks – then with Marshal Ney's corps in support he crossed the Semyenovka stream to attack the Grand Redoubt, the key to the Russian defence. Here Ney and Marshal Junot spearheaded the assault, supported on their left flank by Eugene's troops on the far side of the Kolotchka stream. The battle for the Redoubt was furious, the position being captured and recaptured in bitter hand-to-hand fighting.

By noon Poniatowski had been forced to abandon his assault on the Russian left, while the Russians doggedly held their centre and right, despite debilitatingly heavy losses. Napoleon refused to commit his elite Old Guard, but his Young Guard were eventually sent into the assault on the Russian centre, in an attempt to regain the initiative. The Grand Redoubt fell to a French cavalry assault, and Prince Bagration was mortally wounded, but his men held, regardless of everything Napoleon could throw at them. By late afternoon it was clear that there would be no French victory that day, and by early evening the battle fizzled out as its exhausted survivors withdrew. Both sides lost around 40,000 men that day, but during the night Kutuzov withdrew his battered army. Moscow would fall, but the Russian army would live to fight another day. Napoleon's equally battered Grande Armée, though, was now deep in hostile country, and winter was coming.

LEFT During this costly battle the Grand Redoubt which dominated the Russian centre was a focal point for the fighting. It was finally captured by an assault at 3pm, spearheaded by Saxon cuirassiers. But the battle would drag on until nightfall, by which time both armies had worn themselves out. (Peter Dennis © Osprey Publishing)

LEIPZIG, 16–19 OCTOBER 1813

Napoleon's Grande Armée was almost completely destroyed in the Russian campaign, but somehow he managed to raise an army of 120,000 men. However, by then a new anti-French coalition had been formed by Britain, Prussia, Russia and Sweden. Still, bolstered by his reinforcements, Napoleon would renew the fight in Central Germany. In the spring of 1813 Napoleon inflicted major defeats on the Russo-Prussian army at Lützen and Bautzen, near Dresden. Then, Napoleon agreed to Allied requests for a three-month armistice.

When the fighting resumed in August, Austria had joined the coalition and three allied armies were now in the field. The autumn campaign saw the fortunes of war ebb and flow, but by

September Napoleon had withdrawn to the River Elbe, gathering his forces around Leipzig. The allied armies converged on the city from north, east and south, and by mid-October were poised to attack.

The forces involved were immense. Napoleon now commanded 195,000 men including 23,000 cavalry and 700 guns. These included sizeable German allied contingents. He held the central position, his corps deployed in a ring around Leipzig, their defences anchored on villages. The allies, under the overall leadership of the Austrian Field Marshal Schwarzenberg, had 365,000 men, including over 70,000 cavalry and 1,400 guns. Over half of these troops were Russian, and the rest Austrian, Prussian and Swedish. Some of these, though, had still not reached the battlefield when the fighting began on 16 October.

The 'Battle of the Nations' involved Allied attacks at various points around the semi-circular French perimeter. To the north, the Prussian Field Marshal Blücher pressed Marshal Ney hard, and a desperate see-saw battle saw the key village of Mockern repeatedly changing hands. Meanwhile, Schwarzenberg attacked in the south-west, around the villages of Wachau and Liebertwolkwitz, initiating one of the largest cavalry clashes of the war. By nightfall, though, neither side had made any real headway.

There was little fighting the next day, but battle was resumed on 18 October, after the arrival of Swedish prince Bernadotte's Army of the North. That morning all three allied armies launched large-scale assaults on a reduced French perimeter. Blücher resumed his attack to the north, while Bernadotte attacked from the north-east, where the bulk of Ney's corps had been redeployed to face him. Schwarzenberg's troops attacked all along the southern perimeter, where the bloodiest fighting of the battle took place around the village of Probstheida. Napoleon committed his Old Guard to hold the line, but in mid-afternoon the defection of the Saxons rendered his position untenable. As night fell the French began withdrawing through Leipzig, and the battle-weary allies didn't press them until the following morning. At 1pm, a panicked engineer destroyed the bridge spanning the River Elster, trapping the remnants of the French Army on the wrong side of the river. By then, though, it was clear that Napoleon had suffered an irreversible defeat. His army lost 73,000 in the battle, compared to 38,000 Prussians and Russians, 8,000 Austrians and 200 Swedes. Germany had been lost. Now, Napoleon had to concentrate on saving France itself.

LEFT The sprawling battlefield of Leipzig was dominated by a string of villages, which were used as strongpoints by both armies. One of these was the linked village of Gülden-Gossa, which on 16 October was fought over by the French of General Pacthod's Division and the Russian Imperial Guard. (Mark Stacey © Osprey Publishing)

WATERLOO, 18 JUNE 1815

In 1814 Napoleon and his small French army fought hard to repel the allies from French soil, but despite a string of French victories, Allied numbers prevailed, Paris fell, and on 6 April Napoleon was forced to abdicate. He was exiled to the island of Elba, accompanied by a personal guard of 1,000 men. King Louis XVIII now ruled France, but he was unpopular, and many yearned for the old days. This prompted Napoleon to stage a return. On 29 February 1815, he landed in southern France at the head of his tiny army. As he marched inland soldiers and people rallied to his cause, Louis fled and on 20 April Napoleon entered Paris in triumph.

A new anti-French coalition was formed, and by June the Duke of Wellington's Anglo-Dutch

and Marshal Blücher's Prussians had gathered in Belgium. Napoleon raised a fresh army of his own, gathered on France's northern border. He intended to strike first, driving a wedge between Wellington and Blücher before defeating each army in detail. On 15 June Napoleon's army advanced into Belgium and defeated the Prussians at Ligny. That same day, a detached force under Marshal Ney engaged Wellington at nearby Quatre Bras, but was repulsed. Blücher's defeat, however, made Wellington's position untenable, so he withdrew northwards, and redeployed his army a few miles south of Brussels, where a ridge spanned the Brussels road near the village of Waterloo. Meanwhile, Blücher's army was pursued by Marshal Grouchy, while Napoleon's main army pursued Wellington.

Contact was made on 17 June and, amid torrential rain, both commanders prepared for battle the following morning. Napoleon had 72,000 men and 250 guns at his command; Wellington 67,500 men and 156 guns, most of which were British, supported by Dutch-Belgian, Nassau and Brunswick contingents. But Wellington had deployed on the reverse slope of the ridge, with forward outposts in the farms of Hougoumont, La Haye Sainte and Papelotte. On 18 June Napoleon waited for the ground to dry, before assaulting Hougoumont at 11.30am. The garrison held the fortified farmhouse all day. As Napoleon prepared for his main assault, Prussian troops were spotted to the west. Blücher had evaded Grouchy and had 'marched to the sound of the guns'. Napoleon deployed troops to contain them, then attacked the ridge but was repulsed, as was a counter-charge by British cavalry.

By mid-afternoon Blücher's 43,000 Prussians were attacking Plancenoit in the French right rear, and Napoleon was outnumbered. He left Marshal Ney to deal with Wellington, while he saw to the Prussian threat. In mid-afternoon, Ney unleashed the French cavalry, whose attack on the ridge was repulsed by the British squares. All Ney had gained was control of La Haye Sainte. Then, at 7pm, Napoleon released his Old Guard, to allow time for his army to retire; it was defeated, at which point Wellington ordered a general advance. The demoralized army streamed from the field, leaving Wellington and Blücher to meet on the battlefield. That day the Allies lost 22,000 men, and the French twice that. Napoleon lost France, his title and his freedom. However, as Wellington remarked afterwards: 'it had been a close-run thing'.

LEFT On the afternoon of 18 June the attack of General D'Erlon's French corps threatened Wellington's centre. To ease the pressure, Lord Somerset's Household Brigade charged the French cuirassiers of General Dubois' division, driving them back before being wasted in their own forlorn charge at the French guns. (Gerry Embleton © Osprey Publishing)

THE AGE OF EMPIRES

THE ALAMO, FEBRUARY–MARCH 1836

In 1821 Mexico gained its independence from Spain, and its new government granted citizenship to all its people, including North American settlers. Over the next decade, though, a growing number of North Americans settled in the Mexican province of Texas, either legally, as in the case of a group led there by the empresario Stephen Austin, or illegally. Land speculation abounded, and as the number of Americans grew, so too did tensions with the Mexican authorities. One reason was slavery, outlawed by the Mexican government, but still embraced by many Mexican American colonists – or Texians as they became known. In 1832, an armed insurrection broke out in Texas when the Mexican Army tried to impose the country's

immigration and slavery laws on the Texians. This subsided when the troops withdrew, but tensions remained high. In 1835, Mexico was thrown into chaos by a series of regional revolts against the government. Most of these were eventually supressed, but many Texians saw this larger uprising as their chance to gain their own independence, and in June they rose in another armed insurrection. By the following March the Texians had formed their own Republic.

The Mexican president, General Antonio López de Santa Anna, vowed to subdue the rebels, and led a two-pronged assault on Texas. One force overcame resistance along the coast, while his main army marched on San Antonio de Béxar, the epicentre of the revolt. On 23 February Santa Anna's army reached Béxar, and discovered that the Texians had withdrawn into the nearby Alamo, a former Spanish mission that had been converted into a fort. By evening the Alamo was besieged by the small Mexican army. Santa Anna had around 3,000 regular but poorly trained troops at his disposal, including artillery, while the Texian garrison led by William Travis numbered some 185 to 260 men.

During the opening days of the siege Santa Anna emplaced his light artillery batteries, and began a bombardment of the fort which was largely ineffective. His men also skirmished with the defenders, who made occasional sorties, and sent out a handful of messengers with pleas for other Texians to come to their relief. The lacklustre siege continued until the evening of 5 March, which the defenders took as a sign that an assault was imminent. Sure enough, the assault began at 5.30am on 6 March. Santa Anna had blocked all escape routes from the Alamo, and grouped 1,800 men into four assault columns, which would simultaneously attack the fort from different directions.

The Texian artillery fire and musketry savaged the packed columns, and the first two assaults were repulsed. Travis, though, was killed during the opening minutes of the assault. The other columns managed to scale the northern wall. The outnumbered defenders were driven back into the interior of the compound. The Texians withdrew to the chapel and barracks as the Mexicans flooded into the fort. It took an hour before these were stormed and taken, and the last of the defenders killed or captured. These included the famed frontiersmen James Bowie and Davy Crockett. The Alamo had fallen, at the cost of 400–600 Mexicans killed or wounded. The 13-day defence, though, would inspire other Texians to continue the revolt and eventually gain their independence. In 1845, Texas officially became part of the United States.

LEFT The dawn assault early on 6 August was extremely costly for the attackers, but they finally managed to gain a foothold on the Alamo's outer walls. Although the outnumbered defenders did what they could, superior Mexican numbers prevailed, and the attackers flooded in to the mission compound. (Mark Stacey © Osprey Publishing)

SOLFERINO, 24 JUNE 1859

For a millennium, Italy had been fragmented into several states, some of which had been ruled by external powers such as France, Spain and Austria. By the mid-19th century, though, the nationalist *Risorgimento* movement calling for the unification of Italy had become the dominant force in Italian politics. At that time, most of northern Italy was controlled by Austria. In 1858 France agreed to help the Kingdom of Sardinia and Piedmont to eject the Austrians from the region and to support the *Risorgimento*, so when war broke out between Austria and Sardinia the following spring, a French army fought alongside its new-found Italian ally. Despite blunderings on both sides, on 4 June the allies defeated the Austrians at the Battle of Magenta, and drove

them back towards the east. Four days later the Sardinian king Victor Emmanuel and the French emperor Napoleon III entered Milan in triumph.

The Austrian army was reinforced, though, and the Austrian emperor Franz Joseph I assumed personal command of his troops. Their advance then resumed and a series of small meeting engagements followed in eastern Lombardy as both armies manoeuvred to gain an advantage over their opponents. Then, when the Austrians found the Franco-Sardinian army from Brescia and was strung out to the south of Lake Garda, Franz Joseph decided to cross the River Mincio and attack the enemy before it could concentrate. In fact Napoleon had resumed his advance, and on 24 June the two armies blundered into each other near the small town of Solferino. Each side had roughly 160,000 men on the field, but these forces were scattered over a front of several miles so clashes took place almost randomly. This hindered the concentration of both armies.

As the battle was presided over by two emperors and a king, much was expected of the troops operating under their eyes. The battle that followed, though, was a haphazard affair, which began in the early morning with Sardinian attacks to the north around San Martino which were repulsed by the Austrians under General von Benedeck. Meanwhile the French had managed to concentrate two corps, supported by the Guard, which assaulted the Austrian lines around Solferino and the village of Medole to the south. The Austrians, though, were able to hold their positions throughout the morning.

Then, just after midday, the French Guard broke through the Austrian centre near the cemetery and convent to the north-west of Solferino. That cleared the way for a second French attack which drove the Austrians out of Solferino itself. A second French corps then resumed its attack in the low ground to the south, and the Austrians began to withdraw. Further south the French line had been weakened to allow the concentration around Solferino. Despite this, that afternoon repeated Austrian attacks against the French right flank were repulsed, and here too the Austrians were forced to pull back. By early evening the battle had petered out, with the Austrians withdrawing to their fortresses to the east. Both sides had lost over 12,000 casualties in this gruelling battle, and it was their suffering which prompted one witness, Jean-Henri Dunant, to found the Red Cross. The battle ended the war, and led directly to the unification of Italy in 1871, under King Victor Emmanuel.

LEFT Shortly after noon the French Imperial Guard broke through the Austrian centre, and stormed Solferino. To turn the tide, the Austrian cavalry counter-attacked to the south of the town, but their colourful ranks were quickly torn apart by French rifle fire delivered at point-blank range.
(Peter Dennis © Osprey Publishing)

VOLTURNO, 1860

The dream of *Risorgimento* had grown during the early 19th century, and by 1859 it had come close to becoming a reality. After two Italian Wars of Independence in 1848–49 and 1859, much of northern Italy had been united under King Victor Emmanuel II of Sardinia-Piedmont. Central and southern Italy, though, remained a patchwork of small states, the largest being the Kingdom of Naples and the Papal State. In early 1860, a rebellion broke out in Sicily, as the general and Italian patriot Giuseppe Garibaldi attempted to liberate the island in the name of the *Risorgimento*. At the head of his red-shirted 'Thousand' he defeated the Neapolitan army and liberated Palermo. This turned the tide, as military aid from all over Europe allowed

Garibaldi to turn his 'Thousand' into an army of Italian liberation. By the end of July all of Sicily had been conquered, and Garibaldi turned his attention to the Italian mainland.

In mid-August Garibaldi sent his army across the Strait of Messina to the Italian mainland province of Calabria. The Neapolitan army under the direct command of King Francis II abandoned Naples, which fell on 7 September. Instead, it moved north to establish a defensive line 15 miles to the north, behind the River Volturno. Garibaldi marched his army up to the river to face the Neapolitans. Meanwhile, a Piedmontese army marched south to support Garibaldi by invading the Papal State, so, fearing he would be caught between two *Risorgimento* forces, Francis II decided to attack Garibaldi before the Piedmontese could join him.

On 30 September, with their king at their head, about half of the 50,000-strong Neapolitan army crossed the Volturno on a broad front between Capua and Caserta. A series of assaults on the Garibaldini positions followed, along a 12-mile front, but for the most part the defenders held their ground, or gave it up grudgingly. Capua was captured, though, as was a line of hills to the east which overlooked the river. Here only one Neapolitan column broke through the defenders' lines, but it was halted near the village of Caserta Vecchia. The following day the Neapolitan assault resumed with a major drive from Capua towards Caserta but this was halted by Garibaldi who led a counter-attack near the town of Santa Maria, to the south-east of Capua. However, to the north, on Monte Tifata, his troops had been forced back.

Still, the Neapolitans had been badly mauled in the fighting, and by nightfall the only fresh troops were those defending Capua. On the night of 1–2 October Garibaldi assaulted the town, which was captured after a brisk fight. By dawn the battle was effectively over and it was clear that King Francis' assault had failed. The battered Neapolitan army withdrew downstream to the port of Gaeta, where it was duly besieged. There, Garibaldi and the Peidmontese joined forces, and Garibaldi ceded his conquered territory to King Victor Emmanuel. Thus, by the time Gaeta surrendered the following February, Italy had been united in all but name. Thanks to Garibaldi, and his hard-won defensive victory at the Volturno, a new united Italy had been created, although it would be another decade before all of Italy was fully united.

LEFT For once Garibaldi's troops were on the defensive in the two-day battle, and were hard-pressed by a series of powerful Neapolitan assaults. Here, at the foot of Monte St. Angelo, Garibaldi inspires his men to counter-attack, an assault that drove the enemy back to Capua, and effectively won the day. (Peter Dennis © Osprey Publishing)

FIRST BULL RUN, 21 JULY 1861

The outbreak of the American Civil War in April 1861 was followed by high expectations on both sides, as the Union and Confederate armies gathered. In the Eastern Theatre, the fighting would inevitably take place in Virginia, and it was here that the Confederate army under General P.G.T. Beauregard was mustered. In the north both public and press clamoured for an early resolution of the war, and in July President Lincoln ordered Brigadier General Irvin McDowell to go onto the offensive. When he complained to the army chief that his army was ill-prepared, he was told they were indeed green troops, but so were those of the enemy! Reluctantly then, in mid-July, McDowell advanced as far as Centerville, Virginia. His plan

was to then advance on the Confederate army gathered around Manassas to the south, on the far side of Bull Run Creek. Meanwhile, at Manassas, the outnumbered Beauregard was reinforced with General Johnson's Army of the Shenandoah, which boosted his force to 32,000 men – roughly equal to McDowell's 35,000-strong army.

On 16 July McDowell began a cautious advance to Bull Run, and two days later his army clashed with the Confederates at the fords between Centerville and Manassas. Therefore, abandoning plans for a direct assault, McDowell launched a wide outflanking movement which saw his men cross the creek further upstream at Sudley Ford. This was well above Beauregard's defensive line. These leading Union brigades then advanced south towards the Warrington Turnpike, where on the eastern bank other Union troops were waiting to cross the creek by way of the turnpike's stone bridge. That morning it looked as if the Confederate left flank would be turned; however, General Evans' small Confederate brigade blocked their way, and held its ground until reinforcements could arrive. It took two hours for McDowell's larger force to drive this blocking force back across the turnpike.

This allowed two more Union brigades to cross the creek onto its western bank.

By late morning the Confederate line had re-formed to the south of the turnpike on Henry House Hill. Beauregard was still redeploying his army to the north, with his brigades marching to the sound of the guns. Before they could arrive, though, the Union army resumed its advance, and Henry House Hill became the scene of bitter fighting. The defenders began to falter, but then the first of Beauregard's reinforcements arrived, Jackson's Virginia brigade, which joined the line and held its ground against all-comers. This earned Jackson his nickname 'Stonewall'. The tide of battle turned in favour of the Confederates when the 33rd Virginia Regiment charged and captured a Union battery on the summit of the hill. As the rest of Beauregard's reinforcements arrived, the weary Union troops began to pull back. When Beauregard ordered a general advance, this turned it into a panicked rout as the Union troops fled over the stone bridge to safety. McDowell lost around 3,000 men to Beauregard's 2,000, but the real victory was the boost the battle gave to Confederate confidence. This decisive Confederate victory ended all Union hopes for a quick end to the war.

LEFT In what became a turning point of the battle, at around 2.30pm, defying orders, Colonel Cummings led his 33rd Virginia Regiment in an impetuous charge against the Union guns defending Henry House Hill. The guns were quickly overrun, and the supporting 11th New York Regiment were put to flight. (Peter Dennis © Osprey Publishing)

VICKSBURG, MAY–JULY 1863

Union strategists quickly realized that the most effective way to defeat the Confederacy was to control the Mississippi River. That would cut the nascent country in two, sever its Trans-Mississippi supply lines and reopen the river to northern commerce. This great enterprise began in April 1862 with General Grant's victory at Shiloh on the Tennessee River. That secured most of Tennessee for the Union, and cleared the way for a drive down the Mississippi. With the support of a fleet of riverine ironclads and gunboats, Union forces advanced downriver to Memphis, which fell in June after a naval battle on the river. At the southern end of the Mississippi, in April, the US Navy forced its way past the defences guarding the mouth of the river

and went on to capture New Orleans. Admiral Farragut's fleet then steamed upriver to take Baton Rouge and Natchez. That just left the key port of Vicksburg in Mississippi in Confederate hands, where a railway provided the Confederacy's last link between its eastern and western states.

Vicksburg, though, was heavily fortified, and on 23 May its defenders repulsed an attempt by Farragut to force his way past its defences. He tried again on 28 June and this time his fleet was badly battered but managed to pass the city, to link up with the Union river fleet further upstream. It passed Vicksburg again in mid-July, in pursuit of the Confederate ironclad *Arkansas*, which was eventually destroyed near Baton Rouge. The river secure, Grant's Army of the Tennessee could now begin operations against Vicksburg. That winter, though, all attempts to probe the defences of the city were foiled. These continued into the spring of 1862 but all Grant achieved was to strengthen his hold on the city. By early May, though, he was ready to lay siege to Vicksburg. This was delayed when Lieutenant General John Pemberton, commanding the city's defenders, marched east to sever Grant's lines of supply. Pemberton was defeated, though, at Champions Hill, and four days later Grant began his siege.

An initial Union assault on 19 May was repulsed with heavy losses. This had been made by General Sherman's corps against the north-east corner of Vicksburg's defences. A second assault on 22 May by General McPherson and General McClerland's corps on the defences' eastern perimeter was also rebuffed. Altogether, Grant's army had suffered 3,000 casualties in the two assaults. After that, Grant left it to his artillery to do their work and for the next 48 days Vicksburg was pounded by over 200 guns. The defenders sought cover in caves cut in the bluffs overlooking the river, or in the basements of bombed-out buildings, but they were fast running out of food and were reduced to scavenging for rats.

Grant launched another assault on 25 June after his engineers detonated a mine on the eastern perimeter. McPherson's troops made little headway, though, and the assault was called off. In the end it was starvation that brought Vicksburg to its knees. Unwilling to cause the civilian population further suffering, Pemberton surrendered the city on 4 July. The fall of Vicksburg meant that the Mississippi was completely controlled by the Union. As a delighted President Lincoln put it, 'The father of waters flows again'! Even more importantly the Confederacy was now irrevocably cut in two.

LEFT On the night of 16 April, Admiral Porter's river ironclads steamed downstream past Vicksburg, running the gauntlet of the Confederate guns. The ironclads were protecting several Union transports, which were needed to reinforce General Grant's operations to the south of the city. (Tony Bryan © Osprey Publishing)

GETTYSBURG, 1–3 JULY 1863

Despite extensive campaigning in the Eastern Theatre during 1862, neither side managed to gain a decisive victory. The fighting resumed the following spring, when the Army of the Potomac was bested by General Robert E. Lee at Chancellorsville. This victory encouraged Lee to march north and take the war to the enemy. In early June Lee's army crossed the Potomac River and pressed on through Maryland into Pennsylvania. The Army of the Potomac, now commanded by General Meade, pursued him and in early July the two armies converged on the small Pennsylvania town of Gettysburg. This would be the site of the most important battle of the war.

Lee's veteran Army of Northern Virginia was divided into three corps, commanded by generals

Longstreet, Ewell and A.P. Hill, a total of 72,000 men. They were supported by four divisions of cavalry led by General J.E.B. Stuart. The battle began in the afternoon of 1 July. A division of Hill's corps was approaching Gettysburg from the west when it clashed with a Union cavalry division. The fighting spread as both sides marched to the sound of the guns. However, Lee was unaware that the bulk of Meade's 100,000-strong army was approaching Gettysburg from the east. By evening Hill's men had driven the Union troops back through Gettysburg and onto the high ground to the south of the town. The Union troops established a fishhook-shaped defensive perimeter there, anchored on Cemetery Hill. The Confederates held a curving line to the north and east of this high ground.

The battle proper began the following afternoon as Lee had waited for Longstreet's corps to join him. The Union army had been reinforced too and Meade now had almost 100,000 men in six corps at his disposal. His army also held a strong position which ran from Cemetery Hill and Culp's Hill in the north down to Little Round Top two miles to the south. The Confederate assault began at 4pm when Longstreet's corps advanced on Little Round Top. The attack lost momentum, though, as Longstreet's men became embroiled in a desperate struggle to the east of the high ground. The Confederate assault eventually stalled on the slopes of Little Round Top. To the north, Longstreet's attack was followed by assaults on Cemetery Ridge and Cemetery Hill by A.P. Hill's corps, and an attack on Culp's Hill by Ewell, but in both cases the Union defences proved too strong and the Confederate assaults were repulsed before nightfall.

The following morning Lee tried one last attack. At 3pm, after a preliminary bombardment, he unleashed a frontal assault by 15,000 men from Longstreet and Hill's corps. They were led by General George Pickett, who aimed his men towards the Union lines on Cemetery Ridge. Despite horrendous casualties from Union guns his men pressed on to reach the defenders who were ensconced behind stone walls. Only a few hundred men managed to advance any further, though, and these were quickly cut down or captured. Pickett's survivors retreated, leaving the field strewn with Confederate dead. That evening Lee withdrew his shattered army and led them back into Virginia. Both sides had lost over 23,000 men in the battle, but while Union casualties could be replaced, Confederate losses could not. Gettysburg had been the high-water mark of the Confederate cause. After it, all Lee could do was to hold on as best he could, and so delay the inevitability of a Union victory.

LEFT The fighting on the first day was crucial as it established the ground occupied by the two armies for the main battle the following day. Here, North Carolina and Virginia infantry from General A.P. Hill's Corps assault Union troops from General Reynold's I Corps near McPherson Farm, a mile to the west of Gettysburg. (Steve Noon © Osprey Publishing)

ISANDLWANA, 22 JANUARY 1879

In 1806, at the height of the Napoleonic Wars, the British gained a foothold in southern Africa when they annexed the Cape Colony from the Dutch. During the early 19th century British territories there were expanded to include neighbouring Natal, which brought them into contact with the Boers – white Afrikaner settlers of Dutch extraction – and to several indigenous tribal peoples, the chief of which was the Zulu Kingdom. Neither the Boers nor the Zulus favoured incorporation into Britain's expanding empire, and boundary disputes and incursions increased tensions in the region. In 1878 British officials deliberately provoked a conflict with the Zulus, as they intended to annex Zululand to Britain's South African territories. On 11 January

1879, when the Zulu king Cetshwayo refused to comply with their demands, a British army led by Lord Chelmsford crossed the Buffalo River and invaded Zululand.

Chelmsford deployed his 16,500 troops in three widely separated columns, each with orders to converge on the Zulu capital of Ulundi. His largest force, though, was the central one of 7,800 men, which crossed the river at Rorke's Drift. By 22 January the central column was encamped at Isandlwana, not far from the drift. Chelmsford, though, decided to divide his force and led the bulk of his central column east in search of Cetshwayo. He left a much smaller force of 1,837 men at Isandlwana under the command of Colonel Anthony Durnford and Lieutenant Colonel Henry Pulleine. These included British regulars, plus Natal colonial and indigenous troops. At dawn Chelmsford had set off in pursuit of a Zulu *impi* (army) his scouts had sighted, but it neatly sidestepped the main British column and advanced on Isandlwana. This Zulu *impi* was made up of a dozen regiments of warriors, numbered around 20,000 men, commanded by the *inDuna* (general) Ntshingwayo kaMahole.

That morning local scouts had sighted Zulu regiments close to Isandlwana and raised the alarm. The Zulus launched an immediate attack, with Ntshingwayo deploying his regiments into a buffalo-head formation, its extended flanks resembling the horns. Their task was to envelop the enemy and surround them while the main body engaged them head-on. Pulleine formed his six companies of the 24th Foot into a firing line, and their volleys kept the Zulus at bay – for a time. Other more isolated detachments including a British rocket battery were overrun. However, Durnford, commanding the Natal troops on the British right, was forced to pull back when his men began running out of ammunition. The left Zulu horn closed in, threatening to encircle the defenders. Pulleine then withdrew his regulars into the camp, but casualties mounted, particularly on the flanks of the British line.

A number of indigenous and Natal troops broke and ran, and as the British ammunition ran out, the Zulu horns closed in. In the brutal hand-to-hand fight that followed no quarter was asked or given, as small knots of men fought on until they were cut down. lieutenants Melville and Coghill attempted to save the colours of the 24th Foot, but they died in the attempt. All but a handful of regulars were killed in the fight along with many indigenous and Natal troops – as many as 1,300 men altogether. The Zulus lost around the same number. Isandlwana was an unmitigated disaster for the British Empire, and the news of it was only rendered palatable by the heroic defence of Rorke's Drift a few miles away in the days following the battle.

LEFT During the final stages of the battle the companies of the 24th Foot were pushed back into the British camp by the Zulu centre, at which point their ordered line broke into fragments. Small groups of defenders continued to fight until they were overwhelmed by weight of numbers. (Adam Hook © Osprey Publishing)

SAN JUAN HILL, 1 JULY 1898

Ostensibly, the Spanish-American War of 1898 was fought over the rights of self-determination of the people of Cuba, who had long been in revolt against their Spanish masters. Indirectly, it resulted in Spain losing its colonial empire, and the United States acquiring one themselves. In the United States, public opinion was firmly on the side of the Cubans, so when the battleships USS *Maine* blew up in Havana Harbour on 15 February 1898, most Americans blamed the Spanish. A court of inquiry agreed; therefore, spurred on by the inflammatory American press, war was declared between Spain and the United States.

While an American military expedition was gathered in Tampa, Florida, a small Spanish

squadron sailed from Spain and arrived off the south-eastern port of Santiago de Cuba in late May. A few days later it was blockaded by a significantly more powerful American squadron. On 14 May a fleet of American transports left Tampa with 15,000 troops embarked, under the command of Major-General William Shafter. Although there were 160,000 Spanish troops on Cuba, these had to defend the whole island, with the bulk of them stationed around Havana, so Shafter decided to land near Santiago, to neutralize the Spanish squadron and gain a secure base in eastern Cuba. After that he would see what developed.

On 22 June Shafter's V Corps landed at Daiquiri, to the east of Santiago, and began advancing on the city. Two days later his vanguard skirmished with Spanish troops, whereupon his army encamped some five miles from the Spanish defences. These extended from the fortified village of El Caney in the north to San Juan Hill, immediately to the east of Santiago. Shafter waited there for a week, while supplies were brought up, then resumed his advance. He began his attack by assaulting El Caney. The expectation was this would be an easy victory, but the heavily outnumbered Spanish defenders proved extremely dogged, and it took most of the day for a full US division to overpower them.

The fight at El Caney was still raging when Shafter's remaining troops approached San Juan Hill along trails through thick woods. Their approach, though, was guided by an observation balloon, and from 8.20am a supporting battery opened up a bombardment of the Spanish earthworks on the hill. Eventually the woods ended near the foot of the heights, and the Americans sought what cover they could as they waited for the order to attack. In fact it was Teddy Roosevelt's volunteer 'Rough Riders' who led the assault at 1.15pm, storming the outlying Kettle Hill that protected the main assault from flanking fire. Then, the main assault went in, the Americans braving heavy fire as they charged up the slope to carry the Spanish defences. By 2pm it was over, and the hill was taken. The Americans lost around 1,250 men in the battle and the Spanish 500. The cost to Spain, though, was much greater. With the Americans holding San Juan Hill, Santiago was now untenable, so the Spanish squadron put to sea, only to be annihilated by the waiting American fleet. On 17 July Santiago surrendered, although the war itself would rumble on until the end of the year. In America, the whole conflict was dubbed 'A Splendid Little War', but in fact it firmly established the United States among the leading global powers.

LEFT For the American public, the enduring image of the Spanish–American War was the charge up San Juan Hill by future president Teddy Roosevelt and his 'Rough Riders'. Although a key moment in the battle, it was only one part of the fight, which secured the hill from its Spanish defenders. (Dave Rickman © Osprey Publishing)

TSUSHIMA, 27–28 MAY 1905

In the 1890s the Trans-Siberian Railway reached Vladivostok on the Sea of Japan, giving Imperial Russia access to the Pacific. The Russians then gained permission from the Chinese to extend the railway into Manchuria, which extended their influence into northern China. They went on to gain control of Port Arthur, a Manchurian port which now became the home port of Russia's small Pacific Fleet. In Japan this Russian expansion was seen as a threat to their own sphere of influence in Korea, and so they responded by using British help to strengthen their navy. By February 1904 it looked as if war was inevitable, so the Japanese launched a pre-emptive strike on Port Arthur, which damaged two battleships and a cruiser. Another cruiser

was sunk in Korean waters and, as a result, the Russo-Japanese War (1904–05) was now under way. The Japanese retained the initiative, using minefields and a naval blockade to contain the Russian fleet.

In August, the two fleets clashed at the Battle of the Yellow Sea. Although indecisive, the Russian admiral Vitgeft was killed and his fleet returned to Port Arthur or other neutral ports. To restore the situation the decision was made to reinforce the Russian Pacific Fleet. This, though, had to come from the Baltic, which meant the voyage would take this new fleet halfway around the world. It left the Baltic in October, and after passing through the English Channel it sailed down the coast of West Africa and into the Indian Ocean. Reinforcements reached it via the Suez Canal, and the fleet commander, Admiral Rozhdestvensky, rendezvoused with them at Cam Ranh Bay in Indochina. By then he had learned that Port Arthur had fallen, and the fleet there had been scuttled, so in mid-May he pressed on towards Vladivostok.

At 1.40pm on 27 May the Russians sighted Admiral Togo's Japanese fleet. He had four modern battleships and two armoured cruisers under his command, while Rozhdestvensky's fleet consisted of four modern battleships, five older ones and three coastal defence cruisers. The Japanese ships were generally faster than their Russian counterparts and their crews much better trained. The battle began at 2.10pm, as both sides opened fire at a range of 3½ miles while on parallel courses. The Japanese concentrated on Rozhdestvensky's modern flagship *Kniaz Suvorov*, which was soon badly damaged. Then it was the turn of the battleship *Oslyabya*, which was crippled and pulled out of the Russian line. By 3pm the range had dropped to less than a mile and the pounding continued, with the Russians suffering heavy damage.

Togo skilfully used his ships' superior speed to outmanoeuvre the Russians, and his better gunnery to inflict real punishment on the enemy. The battle became increasingly one-sided as the afternoon wore on and more Russian ships were crippled. By 7pm the modern battleships *Alexander III* and *Borodino* had been sunk, and the rest of the Russian fleet fled towards Vladivostok. The attacks continued through the night, though, as Togo pursued his beaten foes. In the end the Russian fleet was annihilated – only a cruiser and two destroyers reached Vladivostok. The Russians lost six battleships sunk and two captured at Tsushima, plus six other armoured ships and several smaller warships. All the Japanese ships survived the battle. This decisive naval victory humbled Russia, and launched Japan on its course to becoming a world power.

LEFT The Russian fleet was poorly prepared for the battle, and was both outmanoeuvred and outfought. After suffering major losses the battered Russian survivors withdrew, led by Admiral Nebogatov, and the Japanese pursued them. Eventually Nebogatov was forced to order his squadron to surrender. (Peter Dennis © Osprey Publishing)

WORLD WAR I

TANNENBERG, 5–12 SEPTEMBER 1914

On 28 June 1914, the Austrian archduke Franz Ferdinand was assassinated in Sarajevo, triggering a series of diplomatic events which led directly to a worldwide war, where Germany and Austria-Hungary were pitched against Britain, France, Serbia and Russia. As a result, in August 1914, Imperial Germany found itself at war on two fronts. However, its High Command already had a plan in place. The Schlieffen Plan called for the bulk of the army to be sent to the west, to fight France. To the east, it was expected that the Imperial Russian Army would take much longer to mobilize, so it was hoped a small army would be able to hold East Prussia against the Russians while the German Army secured a speedy victory on the Western Front. Until that happened,

General von Prittwitz's German Eighth Army would have to hold the line. For their part the Russians planned an immediate offensive in East Prussia by General von Rennenkamp's First Army and General Samsonov's Second Army. The Russians mobilized far more quickly than the Germans expected, and on 17 August the 'Russian steamroller' began its advance.

There were two offensives, one on each side of the broken terrain of the Masurian Lakes. To the north, Rennenkamp advanced westwards from the frontier towards the fortress city of Königsberg (now Kaliningrad), while to the south Samsonov advanced into East Prussia from Russian-held Poland. As the Germans were outnumbered two to one, the Russians expected the enemy would withdraw ahead of their 'steamroller'. Instead, an advance German corps counter-attacked Rennenkamp at Gumbinnen on 20 August, but the costly battle was indecisive. A worried Prittwitz ordered his army to retreat to the River Vistula, a decision which led to his replacement by the more able General von Hindenburg. Realizing that the cautious Rennenkamp had slowed his advance, Hindenburg decided to concentrate the bulk of his army against Samsonov.

The Second Army had crossed the frontier on 21 August, and was advancing slowly along a broad front. Their use of uncoded radio messages gave Hindenburg's staff a good idea of their deployment, so the German commander decided to concentrate against Samsonov's right flank before the rest of the Second Army could march to its aid. Hindenburg used the railway to speed his concentration, and on 24 August a fast-moving battle of attack and manoeuvre began around the East Prussian towns of Tannenberg – site of the battle of 1410 – and Bischofsburg, 40 miles to the north-east. On both spread-out battlefields each side tried to outmanoeuvre the other, but the Russians were less suited to such a fluid battle, and most of Samsonov's army continued to advance northwards. As a result, its left and right were outmanoeuvred and outflanked, and then cut to pieces. Hindenburg then closed the trap, swinging his flanking corps in on Samsonov's rear. By 30 August it was clear that the Russian Second Army was surrounded, and discipline collapsed in Samsonov's army. The following day the Russian general committed suicide, leaving his army to its fate. In the end, with 50,000 casualties and another 95,000 men captured, it ceased to exist. It was a spectacular German victory, and with it the Russian offensive collapsed. In effect, the Russian steamroller had run out of steam, and now, on the Eastern Front, it was the Germans who held the initiative.

LEFT Although victory at Tannenberg was made possible by German staffwork, mistakes were made. For instance, the attack by the German 35th Division was repulsed by Russian infantry, entrenched in villages such as Mattischkehmen near Gumbinnen which the Germans thought were unoccupied. (Adam Hook © Osprey Publishing)

FIRST MARNE, 5–12 SEPTEMBER 1914

At the outbreak of war the German High Command initiated the Schlieffen Plan, which involved attacking France through neutral Belgium. The bulk of the army would be concentrated on its right wing, which would execute a scythe-like sweep designed to encircle Paris. But the plan had been modified by the German General Staff since its inception in 1905–06, and the right wing of the attack had been significantly weakened. Still, when the invasion began in early August the German Army advanced steadily through Belgium, and Brussels fell on 20 August, then the advance slowed as it encountered British and French blocking forces. By now the main German thrust was along a line of advance from Brussels to

Paris, on a 40-mile front. Three German armies crossed into France around 24 August, despite hard-fought rearguard actions around Mons and Charleroi. This was followed by 'The Great Retreat', as the Allies fell back 70 miles to the River Marne. Hasty preparations were made to defend Paris. On 3 September the French government left the city and moved to Bordeaux.

By then, though, the mood in the army had changed. The retreat had ended, and the Allies were now formed up in a strong defensive position behind the River Marne. The French Sixth Army defended Paris, just 20 miles from the front line, while General French's British Expeditionary Force (BEF) was deployed to the east of the city. Two more French armies extended the defensive line eastwards as far as Verdun including General Foch's newly formed French Ninth Army. On the German side, General von Kluck's First Army had crossed the Marne and now faced the British between Meaux and Sézanne, but they had advanced ahead of General von Bülow's Second Army, which was now behind Kluck's left flank. Kluck's right flank was therefore exposed. The French commander-in-chief General Joffre realized this and laid plans for an immediate counter-attack.

LEFT The most famous incident in the battle involved 'The Taxis of the Marne'. On the night of 6–7 September, some 600 Parisian taxis were used to transport two regiments of the French Sixth Army to the front line near Nanteuil, 25 miles from the city, and so prevent the Germans taking the town. (Graham Turner © Osprey Publishing)

On 5 September the Allied counter-offensive began, spearheaded by General Gallieni's Sixth Army. In one of the most famous incidents of the war, some 600 Parisian taxis were used to ferry 4,000 French troops of the Paris garrison to Nateuil-en-Haudoin north of Meaux, and these spearheaded Galliéni's drive into Kluck's exposed flank and rear. The German commander responded by redeploying his army to face this new threat, which in turn widened the gap between him and Bülow's army. The following day the BEF and the French Fifth Army advanced northwards to occupy the gap, completely isolating Kluck from the rest of the German armies. By the evening of 7 September Kluck's left flank had been driven back over the Marne, as the French Fifth Army recaptured Château-Thierry, an advance of 25 miles in two days.

The German commander-in-chief Count von Moltke (the younger) now realized that he risked losing Kluck's entire army, and possibly Bülow's army as well. Late on 8 September he ordered both commanders to withdraw, or risk disaster. This retreat continued until 12 September, by which time the Germans were north of the River Aisne. This effectively ended the Germans' drive on Paris, and any hope of a quick victory on the Western Front. The fighting along the Marne had cost both armies a staggering 250,000 casualties, but this was far from the end of the slaughter. It simply hastened the move towards the horrors of trench warfare.

VERDUN, FEBRUARY–DECEMBER 1916

By the end of 1914 the Western Front had stagnated as both sides took to the trenches which stretched from the Belgian coast to the Swiss frontier. This front remained largely static throughout 1915, despite several costly and unsuccessful Allied attempts to break the deadlock. For 1916, the French commander General Joffre planned to wear the Germans down, before launching his own offensive in the spring. Instead, it was the Germans who seized the initiative, as General von Falkenhayn, the Chief of the German General Staff, launched a new kind of battle. This involved launching an overwhelming attack on a limited sector of the front, then hold his gains against French counter-attacks. His intention was to 'bleed France dry'.

The sector he chose was the heavily fortified city of Verdun on the River Meuse.

Falkenhayn's offensive began on 21 February 1916 with a massed assault by Crown Prince Wilhelm's German Fifth Army preceded by a lengthy bombardment by over 800 guns. Within three days the Germans had advanced up to four miles, but the cost for both sides had been high. The main French fortress of Fort Douaumont was captured, and several other key defensive positions on the eastern bank of the River Meuse. However, French reinforcements were rushed to the front and the French line held. The French commander of the sector, General Pétain, ordered that there would be no further retreat, and he launched a series of counter-attacks, one of which briefly recaptured Fort Douaumont.

Pétain also reorganized the French defences and his supply line, dubbed the *Voie Sacrée* ('Sacred Way') by his men. The Germans, though, were equally adept at attacking, and in June they captured another key position, Fort Vaux, thanks to the use of flamethrowers and phosgene gas shells. The Germans had now come within two miles of Verdun itself. In March they launched a major attack to the west of the Meuse, but the French line was stabilized and anchored on the now blood-soaked hill known as *Le Mort Homme* ('The Dead Man'). It was captured by the Germans in May, however, then recaptured by the French in August, both at a huge human cost. By now the Verdun battlefield was a morass of mud, water-filled shell-holes and decomposing bodies, but despite the horrendous conditions the brutal fight raged unabated with attack and counter-attack bleeding both armies of men.

The Somme offensive in July led to the Germans redirecting men there, and the Verdun offensive was halted. Then in mid-October the French launched a major offensive of their own, preceded by a creeping barrage by hundreds of guns. Fort Douaumont was retaken on 24 October, and Fort Vaux nine days later. A second French offensive in December saw the Germans driven back to their start lines of ten months before. The Battle of Verdun was over, and while it was now technically a French victory, the human cost was staggering. Over a third of a million French soldiers were killed or wounded at Verdun, and almost as many German ones – all for almost no territorial gain. Although the war would continue, Verdun would be remembered as the most horrific mass slaughter of the conflict.

LEFT The fighting around Verdun was horrific, involving a horrendous slaughter on an industrial scale. While artillery bombardments and machine-gun fire accounted for most of the casualties, the flamethrower, used here by German troops, was the most feared weapon on the Verdun battlefield. (Steve Noon © Osprey Publishing)

THE BATTLE OF JUTLAND, 31 MAY 1916

Throughout the 19th century, the British had enjoyed unchallenged naval supremacy. So, when the German Kaiser Wilhelm III began building a rival fleet, the British saw this as a threat. The 'naval arms race' is seen as one of the factors which led to the outbreak of war in 1914. The German High Seas Fleet lacked the strength to directly challenge the British Grand Fleet; therefore, it remained a 'fleet in being', its presence forcing the British to maintain their own fleet in the North Sea. During the opening years of the war, the two fleets did little more than skirmish. Then, in late May 1916, Vice Admiral Scheer, commander of the High Seas Fleet, put to sea again, this time heading north towards the Skagerrak, the exit from the Baltic

between Denmark and Norway. The main battle fleet of 16 dreadnoughts and six pre-dreadnought battleships was preceded by a powerful scouting group of five battlecruisers, under the command of Vice Admiral Hipper. When news of the sortie reached Admiral Jellicoe, commander of the Grand Fleet, he led his ships out of Scapa Flow in Orkney, hoping to intercept Scheer before he could return to his base. From Rosyth, Vice Admiral Beatty's Battlecruiser Fleet also headed east with six battlecruisers to rendezvous with Jellicoe's battle fleet off the Danish coast. In the early afternoon of 31 May Beatty and Hipper's forces made contact, and the rival battlecruisers closed for battle.

By 4pm the two lines of battlecruisers were fighting a duel with each other as they steamed south. Beatty had by far the worst of the duel, losing the battlecruisers *Queen Mary* and *Indomitable*, both blown up when their poorly protected magazines were hit. Hipper's 'run to the south', as this became called, was designed to draw Beatty towards Scheer's battle fleet which was steaming north. Spotting the trap, Beatty turned about and ran north, covered by four powerful fast battleships. Now it was the Germans' turn to be drawn onto the British

battle fleet. By 6pm Jellicoe had deployed his 24 dreadnoughts into line, and 15 minutes later he sighted the High Seas Fleet, steaming directly towards his waiting line. This meant he had 'crossed the T' of the Germans and most of his ships' guns could bear on the enemy, while only the bow guns of the leading German ships could fire back. Scheer faced annihilation, so he ordered a *Gefechtskehrtwendung* – a simultaneous reversal of course by his entire battle fleet.

By now smoke and mist obscured both fleets, so Scheer turned to the east, hoping to escape Jellicoe. Instead, he ran into the British again and had to perform another *Gefechtskehrtwendung* to escape trouble, covered by a massed torpedo boat attack that didn't hit anything but forced Jellicoe to break contact. As dusk fell the two fleets ran south, but the British were now between the Germans and the safety of Kiel. Scheer attempted to break past the British in the dark, and around midnight he succeeded, although he clashed with British destroyers during the breakout. Jellicoe had hoped to renew the battle at dawn, but found that Scheer had escaped. It had been a costly battle for the British, losing three battlecruisers to one German one, plus a German pre-dreadnought battleship. Both sides claimed victory, but strategically the battle was a clear British victory. Jellicoe still controlled the North Sea and continued his blockade of German ports. This, more than anything else, forced the Germans to sue for peace two years later.

LEFT Jutland saw the clash of more firepower than any previous battle in history. Here, the British dreadnoughts *Canada*, *Royal Oak* and *Superb* are pictured at 18.30, firing their main guns at the German battlecruisers to the south, which are driven back by the sheer weight of the British fire. (Howard Gerrard © Osprey Publishing)

THE SOMME, 1 JULY 1916

In the winter of 1915–16, the Allied leaders agreed to launch a series of large-scale offensives in 1916, involving simultaneous attacks by the British, French, Russian and Italian armies. In the end, though, these plans were stymied by the German attack on Verdun in February 1916, which placed increasingly heavy demands on France's military resources. It was originally intended that a summer offensive in the valley of the River Somme would be a predominantly French operation, which the British would support. Now, as the situation in Verdun became increasingly critical, General Joffre, commanding the French Army, requested that his British counterpart General Haig should launch the Somme offensive earlier than planned, in order

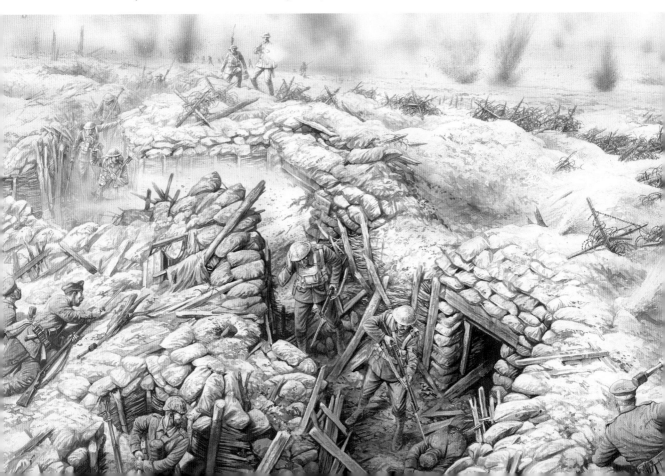

to to take pressure off the embattled French armies at Verdun. Consequently, the resulting Battle of the Somme would be a British operation, with only limited French support on its southern flank.

This sector of the German line was held by seven divisions of General von Below's Second Army, who were well dug in with three lines of defence. The British attack would be carried out by General Allenby's Third Army and General Rawlinson's Fourth Army, a total of 18 divisions, supported by almost 3,000 guns. The attack was earmarked for 1 July, and would take place between the villages of Gommecourt in the north and Dompierre in the south. To the south, a limited French attack would be made by another five divisions drawn from the French Sixth Army. A week before 'H-Hour', the British and French guns opened up a fearsome bombardment, which continued unabated for seven days. It was expected that this would destroy most of the German front-line defences and cut the dense fields of barbed wire in front of their trenches. Instead, although parts of the German line were wrecked, most of it remained intact, including the bunkers where the German troops sheltered.

At 7.30am on 1 July, 18 British divisions attacked along a 20-mile front. However, the Germans, forewarned by intercepted signals, were waiting for them. German machine-gun and rifle fire cut swathes through the attacking ranks, helped by the British instructions to walk rather than to charge. One territorial division, the 36th, lost 3,600 men in the space of ten minutes. A few groups reached the German lines, but these were swiftly overwhelmed by German counter-attacks. By nightfall, over 20,000 British troops had been killed and over 37,000 wounded. By contrast German casualties were just over 10,000 men. The southern portion of the line and the French sector beyond it made some limited gains, though, and the assault was renewed the following day. In fact, the Battle of the Somme would continue until 18 November. For both sides the Somme became a battle of attrition, with horrendous casualties lost in return for extremely meagre gains. By November, the deepest penetration in the battlefield was five miles – achieved at the cost of 620,000 casualties. Nevertheless, the Germans lost 465,000 men themselves. It was a futile slaughter of lives on both sides that has remained a byword for the horror of war ever since.

LEFT While many of the British assaults on the first day of the Somme proved a costly failure, there were some successes. In the north, the British 31st Division captured the Heidenkopf stronghold, but these gains proved temporary, and by nightfall the German defences there had been recaptured. (Peter Dennis © Osprey Publishing)

CAMBRAI, 20–21 NOVEMBER 1917

The immense slaughter of Verdun and the Somme merely marked the start of the war of attrition fought on the Western Front. In 1917 the same strategies were repeated, with a French spring offensive along the River Aisne near Rheims, and a matching British one near Arras. Both achieved little, other than the very costly capture of Vimy Ridge by the Canadians. The Aisne offensive also led to a widespread mutiny in the French Army, as the men of 54 divisions refused to resume the offensive. In the summer, an even more bloody offensive by the British at Passchendaele near Ypres cost the army 300,000 casualties for a gain of less than two miles. The British commander Field Marshal Haig was desperate to break the stalemate, so when

Lieutenant Colonel Elles, commander of the newly formed Royal Tank Corps, offered him a plan, he quickly saw its potential.

The British-designed 'tank' was originally called the 'landship', an armoured tracked vehicle which in theory was invulnerable to machine-gun fire. The new name was introduced to preserve secrecy, as prototypes resembled contemporary steel water tanks. They made their debut on the battlefield in mid-September 1916, when they proved useful, although with a lack of mechanical reliability. In 1917 they were used at Messines Ridge where they worked well, and at nearby Passchendaele, where they bogged down in the Flanders mud. What Elles proposed was to deploy the improved Mark IV version of the tank en masse, on a battlefield where the ground was suitably firm. He and Haig settled on Cambrai, weakly held by units of the German Second Army. This assault would involve 474 Mark IV tanks, supported by infantry, artillery and aircraft, with massed cavalry held in reserve to exploit the expected breakthrough 'to the green fields beyond'.

The assault began at dawn on 20 November, when the tanks, led by Elles himself, appeared out of the mist. Amazingly, the attack achieved total surprise, and thanks to Elles' leadership it went well. He had equipped the lead tanks with wooden fascines to drop in the German trenches to serve as a makeshift bridge. While this was being done, a supporting tank would spray the trench line with machine-gun fire, then the tanks would cross over, allowing the infantry to mop up the defenders. By noon the first two German lines had been captured along a six-mile stretch of the front. By nightfall the third defensive line had been taken, and the tanks had advanced for five miles behind the initial front. However, they were still plagued by mechanical problems, and when they stopped they proved vulnerable to artillery fire. By nightfall over half were out of action.

Another problem was the inability of the infantry to properly support the tanks, and the tanks themselves were unable to take key bunkers and other defensive strongpoints. The cavalry was unable to exploit the success, and the Germans were quick to rush reinforcements to the front. In the end the Cambrai was a limited success, as the British were unable to seize the opportunities presented by the tanks. A few weeks later a German counter-attack recaptured much of the ground which had been won. The tank, though, had proved it had merit as a battlefield weapon – if only a way could be found to really make use of it.

LEFT The first large-scale operational proved a moderate success, spearheading the capture of four successive German defensive lines. They also gave the supporting infantry greater confidence, but it was soon found that the machines were prone to breakdowns, and vulnerable to artillery fire. (Peter Dennis © Osprey Publishing)

AMIENS, 8–12 AUGUST 1918

In the spring of 1918, the Germans launched Operation *Michael*, a series of attacks on the Western Front designed to drive the Allies back towards Paris. The collapse of Imperial Russia's army allowed the Germans to transfer large numbers of men from the east, and this, combined with their new *Stosstruppen* ('stormtrooper') tactics, helped revitalize the campaign. In the end, though, the beleaguered British halted the German offensive in front of Amiens, while the French did the same along the Aisne and Marne. The arrival of the Americans had helped to rejuvenate the Allies, as had the arrival of British Empire troops to reinforce the exhausted British. By contrast the Germans had now expended their advantage in numbers, and their battered armies were becoming increasingly

demoralized. By August, the new Allied supreme commander Marshal Foch and the British and Empire commander Field Marshal Haig agreed that the time had come to launch a large-scale counter-attack, designed to break the will of the German Army.

The Allies led the Germans to believe the British would attack in Flanders, and the French near Rheims. Instead, in total secrecy, Haig concentrated General Byng's Third Army and General Rawlinson's Fourth Army in French Picardy, to the east of Amiens. To the south, similar preparations were made by General Debeney's French First Army. It was the French who struck first, though, in late July, when they drove the Germans back from the Marne to the Aisne, and so out of artillery range of Paris. In early August it was the turn of Haig. Facing him was General von der Marwitz' Second Army with ten under-strength divisions. By contrast Haig had 32 divisions at his command –12 French, ten British, five Australian, four Canadian and one American supported by artillery, tanks and aircraft.

The assault began at dawn on 8 August. This time there would be no pre-attack bombardment. The guns would support the infantry advance, as would tanks and ground-attack aircraft, the aim being to take the German defenders by surprise. These tactics worked perfectly, helped greatly by a heavy mist. By mid-morning the initial German trench lines were captured with relatively light casualties, and a second wave of fresh Allied troops passed through the first wave, to take up the attack. By late morning the Australian and Canadian divisions in the centre of the battlefield had advanced over five miles. Once the front line had been breached the advance continued through the German rear areas. One surprised German divisional headquarters was even captured as it was having a late breakfast.

The attacks in the north along the River Somme were less successful, but further south a 15-mile section of the front had been breached and the Germans pushed back up to eight miles. Allied losses that day were placed at 8,000–10,000 men, while the Germans lost 30,000 plus another 16,000 captured. Over the following days the Allied advance continued, but without the element of surprise the pace of advance slowed. German reinforcements were also brought in to plug the gap in the front line. Still, by 12 August when Haig called off the assault, his men had advanced up to 12 miles and, more significantly, had captured over 50,000 German soldiers, many of whom were eager to surrender. It is little wonder General Ludendorff, German chief-of-staff, called 8 August 'a black day for the German Army'. Essentially, these mass surrenders were only the beginning. Amiens marked the start of the collapse of the German Army.

LEFT At Amiens the aggressive use of Allied tanks and ground-attack aircraft proved decisive, and the German defenders were unable to prevent a breakthrough. Their only real successes came when the tanks advanced too far ahead of their supporting infantry, and could be attacked by stormtroopers. (Peter Dennis © Osprey Publishing)

WARSAW, 13–20 AUGUST 1920

After its defeat at Tannenberg in 1914 the Russian Army was on the defensive on the Eastern Front, and was consistently outmanoeuvred and outfought by the Germans and, to a lesser extent, their Austro-Hungarian allies. By the end of the year the Russians had been driven out of Poland. Russian attempts to counter-attack in 1916 and 1917 ended in failure, and while morale collapsed in the army, increasing war-weariness and shortages at home led to growing political unrest. The abdication of Tsar Nicholas II in March 1917 did little to stabilize the situation, nor did further German advances which almost reached Petrograd, now St. Petersburg. In March 1918 the new Bolshevik government signed the Treaty of Brest-Litovsk,

which effectively ended Russia's involvement in the war, and although much of Russia remained occupied, the Bolsheviks could now concentrate on securing victory in the Russian Civil War.

The end of World War I also saw the emergence of Poland as an independent country. The Poles then took advantage of the vacuum created by the withdrawal of German troops to occupy Lithuania and large swathes of Belarus and parts of Ukraine. The impetus for this was the country's new leader, Marshal Pilsudski, who wanted to restore Poland's 18th-century borders. This, though, coincided with the emergence of the Red Army, forged by Leon Trotsky in the crucible of the Russian Civil War. By the summer of 1919 the Red Army had largely crushed the Ukrainians, and now faced the Poles in Belarus and western Ukraine. Effectively, Poland and the Russian Soviet Republic were now at war. In April 1920 the Poles launched a pre-emptive strike in Belarus which achieved little, but in Ukraine the Poles and their new-found Ukrainian allies captured Kiev. However, the city fell to a Red Army counter-attack in May.

This Red Army counter-offensive was led by General Budyonny, whose 1st Cavalry Army swept the Poles back to Lvov (now Lviv in Ukraine). In July another Red Army offensive led by General Tukhachevsky recaptured Belarus. By early August, Budyonny and Tukhachevsky had driven the Poles back to within 20 miles of Warsaw. Both sides were exhausted, but Tukhachevsky was ordered to renew the offensive. It began on 13 August, with the two Russian army groups driving west towards Warsaw, supported to the south by a cavalry army. The Poles, though, led by Pilsudski, came up with a daring plan. The defences of Warsaw were stripped of men, and those who remained were ordered to hold on. Instead, Pilsudski concentrated his troops on Budyonny's southern flank. Intelligence reports suggested that the Russian offensive was bound to stall in front of Warsaw due to a chronic lack of supplies. When it did, on 16 August, Pilsudski struck the exposed flank of the Red Army with 57,000 fresh Polish troops. The capture of the town of Radzymin east of Warsaw marked the end of any Russian threat to Warsaw. Tukhachevsky tried to regroup his army groups, but his radios were jammed by the Poles. By 20 August the Red Army was in full retreat, and the Poles pursued them almost to the gates of Kiev. Both armies suffered around 25,000 casualties, but the Red Army also lost another 65,000 who were captured during the chaotic retreat. In October an armistice was agreed, bringing the Russo-Polish War to an end. Effectively, Poland's independence had been won in the battle for Warsaw.

LEFT During the Red Army's drive west, the mobility of Budyonny Cavalry Army proved decisive. Here, the Bolshevik horsemen attack a Polish trench line near Kiev. Eventually, though, the Polish General Pilsudski used the same aggressive tactics against the Soviets in the battle before Warsaw. (Steve Noon © Osprey Publishing)

WORLD WAR II

SEDAN, 12–15 MAY 1940

Following the outbreak of war in September 1939, France and Britain waited for a German assault that never materialized. But the 'phoney war' ended abruptly in April 1940, when the Germans invaded Denmark and Norway. It took a day to conquer Denmark, and two months to subdue Norway, which was supported by French and British troops. Then, on 10 May, the Germans launched *Fall Gelb* ('Case Yellow'), the invasion of France. The French had placed a lot of faith in the Maginot Line, the formidable defences protecting its eastern border. However, the Germans avoided launching a direct attack on it, and instead sent their armies through neutral Belgium, Luxembourg and the Netherlands. On paper the two sides were fairly

equal – 130 Allied divisions facing 140 German ones. The Allies had more tanks, and the Belgians and Dutch added another 32 divisions to the Allied order of battle, but this didn't take into account Germany's preponderance of aircraft, and its new *Blitzkrieg* ('lightning war') tactics.

When the invasion began, the bulk of the Allied divisions in the north marched into Belgium, where the outnumbered Belgians were being driven back towards Brussels. To the south lay the virtually impregnable Maginot Line, which only faced probing attacks. In between, where the French border along the River Meuse faced the heavily wooded Ardennes region of south-eastern Belgium and Luxembourg, the defences were thinly manned. After all, Marshal Pétain had declared the rugged Ardennes 'impenetrable' to a modern army. Therefore, the key town of Sedan on the Meuse was held by a single French division. Unknown to the French, though, the main thrust of Field Marshal von Rundstedt's Army Group A would be deliberately directed through the Ardennes. Spearheading this attack was General Kleist, commanding two well-equipped Panzer corps. His objective was to cross the Meuse at Sedan.

It took less than three days for the head of Panzergruppe von Kleist to pass through the Ardennes and sweep aside the Franco-Belgian troops stationed there. Then, late on 12 May, it crossed the French border a few miles to the north-east of Sedan. Leading the way was General Guderian's XIX Panzer Corps, with the 1st, 2nd and 10th Panzer Divisions, supported by the Grossdeutschland Regiment of motorized infantry. The battle for Sedan began the following morning as the Luftwaffe bombed the French fortifications in a rolling bombardment which lasted until mid-afternoon, with over 500 sorties being flown. Then Guderian advanced towards the Meuse.

At 4pm his Panzergrenadiers used rubber boats to cross the river to the north and south of Sedan, at Donchery, Glaire and Wadelincourt. The assault was covered by fire from the eastern bank, and casualties were light, except at Donchery where the initial attack was driven back. By evening, though, the Germans had secured a bridgehead on the south bank, and German pioneers began building three pontoon bridges, while Sedan itself was cleared of its defenders. Resistance from the reservists of the French 55th Division had crumbled away in the face of the massed air attacks. During the early hours of 14 May German tanks were rolling south from the river, bypassing the line hastily thrown up by the French at Chéchéry. Now, nothing could stop the German panzers as they drove eastwards across France, towards the Channel ports.

LEFT Early on 14 May a pontoon bridge was built across the Meuse north of Sedan, and soon after dawn tanks began crossing it. Allied attempts to bomb the bridges proved unsuccessful, and so the German panzers were able to push on westwards into France. (Peter Dennis © Osprey Publishing)

THE BATTLE OF BRITAIN, JULY–OCTOBER 1940

Following the defeat of France in June 1940, the German High Command hoped that Britain would sue for peace. When this didn't happen, Hitler ordered his commanders to begin plans for Operation *Sealion*, the invasion of Britain. As a prelude to this, the Luftwaffe were ordered to overpower the Royal Air Force (RAF). With complete air superiority, the Luftwaffe could then deal with the Royal Navy, and then support the army's amphibious landings on England's southern coast.

This meant that everything depended on the aerial campaign – the first time in history where a battle between two rival fleets of aircraft would have a direct strategic impact on the outcome of the war. The Luftwaffe, though, had had little

time to recover from its recent losses over France, and it now had 700 Me 109 and Me 110 fighters available to match a similar number of RAF Spitfires and Hurricanes. However, the Luftwaffe would also use its powerful bomber fleets to attack Britain's airfields and air defences during the campaign. Nevertheless, the British had a great advantage in RDF (or radar) which gave RAF Fighter Command warning of German attacks.

The plan devised by Herman Göring, commander-in-chief of the Luftwaffe, was to overpower RAF Fighter Command as quickly as possible. Then the bombers would be used to pound military targets in southern England in advance of the invasion. Daily skirmishes between the two air forces began in late June, as the Luftwaffe attacked shipping in the English Channel and probed British air defences. This was then followed by an overwhelming air assault codenamed *Adlerangriff* ('Eagle Attack'), the objective of which was to destroy Fighter Command by attacking its airfields, radar chains and command centres. *Adlertag* ('Eagle Day') was 13 August. Initial attacks on coastal radar stations and airfields were followed by attacks on airfields further inland

Due to poor weather, it was 18 August before the Luftwaffe could deploy all its squadrons, but then, for two weeks, the attacks were relentless. However, on 7 September, following a directive from Hitler, the German bombers were ordered to concentrate on bombing London. The 'Blitz' was certainly devastating for the city and its people, but it gave the RAF a much-needed reprieve. By 1 October these bombing attacks had been switched from day to night-time raids, and were cancelled altogether on 31 October. This, effectively, brought the world's first air campaign to an end.

Throughout the battle, radar gave the British a huge advantage. The chain of radar stations was able to give Fighter Command advance warning of any German attack, and fighters could be scrambled to intercept. Radar allowed the RAF to use their fighters sparingly, and make sure they were placed where they were needed most. Fighters could also be pulled back from airfields under threat and placed out of range of the German fighters. Throughout this assault, Göring was told that the RDF was close to collapse, but in fact the radar stations and almost all of the airfields remained operational all through the campaign. Another advantage was that the British could repair planes or build new ones, and train more pilots faster than the Germans could. Losses on both sides were high – around 1,700 British and 1,950 German aircraft destroyed, roughly equivalent to the starting strengths of the two air forces. The real impact, though, was that Germany had suffered its first major defeat of the war.

LEFT By mid-September the Luftwaffe was convinced it was winning its war of attrition against the Royal Air Force so, on 15 September, when a force of 114 bombers approached London, the Germans were shocked to find themselves under attack from a 'Big Wing' of more than 100 fighters. (Graham Turner © Osprey Publishing)

TARANTO, 11 NOVEMBER 1940

On 10 June, exactly a month after the German invasion of France, Italy entered the war as Germany's ally. This immediately plunged Britain's Mediterranean Fleet into a naval war with the powerful Italian fleet, the Regia Marina. This long and hard-fought campaign was dominated by geography. Britain maintained bases at either end of the Mediterranean, at Gibraltar and Alexandria, and one in its centre on the island of Malta. Maintaining sea routes from Gibraltar to Malta and Egypt became the primary concern for the British fleet's commander, Admiral Cunningham. The Italians had relatively short sea lanes to protect, running between Italy itself and its ports in North Africa, where the Italian Army faced the British along the Libyan–Egyptian border.

Inevitably then, naval clashes would take place along these sea routes, as both sides sought to protect their convoys.

The Italians, though, were better placed for this, with numerous air bases in southern Italy, North Africa and Sicily at their disposal, and a major naval base at Taranto in southern Italy, virtually astride the sea route between Malta and Alexandria. Apart from Malta, whose few fighters were busy protecting the island from Italian bombers, air cover for the British fleet was provided by a single aircraft carrier. Initially, the naval campaign only involved one naval surface clash in July, off Calabria, when the Italians broke off the action after one of their battleships was damaged. Cunningham quickly realized that unless he could neutralize the powerful Italian battle fleet, he would be hard-pressed to keep Malta supplied, or to maintain the vital sea route to Egypt.

Cunningham's solution was to use the newly arrived aircraft carrier *Illustrious* to carry out an air strike on the Italian fleet as it lay in Taranto harbour. This type of daring attack had never been attempted before, so its success was far from guaranteed. The attack was part of a much more complex operation, codenamed *MB-8*, which involved the running of three convoys through the Central Mediterranean to Malta, supported by a large portion of the Mediterranean Fleet. *Illustrious* was the flagship of Rear Admiral Lyster, an advocate of aggressive air strikes of this kind. As the convoy operations were completed successfully, Lyster's carrier headed into the Ionian Sea, accompanied by a small escort. By the evening of 11 November *Illustrious* reached its launching position, 189 miles south-east of Taranto. At 8.30pm a first wave of 12 Swordfish torpedo bombers took off and headed towards the port.

The attack began at 11.10pm. The biplanes approached the anchorage from the south, with some planes dropping flares to illuminate the targets, and the rest dropping down to launch their torpedoes at the six Italian battleships. They then flew off, pursued by heavy anti-aircraft fire. An hour later, at 12.10am, the second wave of just seven Swordfish arrived and repeated the attack before flying off. Both attacks took less than half an hour to complete, and by 2.50am the Swordfish were back aboard *Illustrious*. Later that day a reconnaissance flight from Malta flew over Taranto, and reported the result. One battleship, the *Conte di Cavour* was sunk, and two more, *Littorio* and *Caio Duilio* were crippled and beached. The attackers lost two aircraft. It was a stunning achievement, depriving the Italians of half their battle fleet in a single stroke. It also proved the worth of naval air strikes – a year before the Japanese repeated the whole operation on a much bigger scale at Pearl Harbor.

LEFT The Fleet Air Arm's attack on the Italian battle fleet at Taranto ushered in a new age of warfare. By sinking three battleships, half of Italy's total force, the attack not only evened the odds in the naval battle for the Mediterranean, but demonstrated that the age of naval air power had finally arrived. (Peter Dennis © Osprey Publishing)

MOSCOW, 30 SEPTEMBER–5 DECEMBER 1941

On 22 June 1941 the Germans and their Axis allies launched Operation *Barbarossa* – the invasion of the Soviet Union. This immense undertaking involved over 3.8 million troops, over 3,500 tanks and 5,000 aircraft. The German High Command had studied Napoleon's invasion of Russia in 1812, and knew that they had to destroy the bulk of the Soviet army before it could withdraw into the vastness of the Soviet interior. For the most part this worked perfectly, with dramatic sweeping advances, and the encirclement and destruction of Soviet forces. One encirclement at Minsk a week into the invasion resulted in the capture of 280,000 Soviet troops. The Axis advance was made on an immensely broad front, from the Baltic to the Black Sea, and by mid-July

the German panzers had reached Novgorod in the north, Smolensk in the centre, and Kiev and Odessa in the Ukraine.

Inevitably, though, the pace of advance slowed as the panzers outstripped the German infantry and the Soviet road and rail network proved inadequate to the task of resupplying the forward units. Soviet resistance was hardening too, as reinforcements replaced the troops lost in the frontier battles, but the Axis advance continued as did the German successes. By September, as the Germans approached Leningrad and cut off the Crimea, the commanders in the centre were preparing for a final push towards Moscow, which was codenamed Operation *Typhoon*. Hitler had insisted on the capture of Moscow as the pinnacle of the campaign, despite the coming of the autumn rains, when the USSR's unmetalled roads turned to mud. Three Panzer armies under Generals Hoth, Hoepner and Guderian had been earmarked for the operation, while in front of them, in General Zhukov's West Front, fresh reinforcements taken from the Far East had been used to bolster his defences.

On 30 September the three panzer armies smashed through the Soviet front line, with Hoth and Hoepner encircling a large Soviet army at

Vyazma, and Guderian achieving the same to the south at Bryansk. Around 700,000 Soviet troops were captured. By mid-October Kalinin, Kaluga and Orel had fallen, but then the pace of the German advance slowed, bogged down in the mud, and in the face of Soviet counter-attacks. Nevertheless, on 13 October the Germans reached the hastily constructed Mozhaisk Line, astride the Smolensk to Moscow road. Here, just 65 miles from central Moscow, the equally hastily assembled Soviet defenders waited for the onslaught. The battle that followed was brutal, but in a series of costly frontal attacks the Germans gradually pushed the defenders back. Then the assault was halted due to a lack of supplies.

The lull lasted for two weeks as the Germans regrouped, with the offensive resuming on 15 November, when the ground was frozen enough to allow the panzers to advance. This time the Germans attempted a pincer attack, advancing on Moscow from the north-west and south. By 25 November, though, Hoth had stalled at Kryukovo in the north and Guderian at Kashira in the south. A counter-attack drove Guderian back, but an assault by Hoepner in the centre reached Golitsyno on 1 December, where his men could actually see Moscow. Three days later, though, they were driven back. By this time, the coming of the winter snows effectively ended the battle, and Moscow was saved. The fighting had cost both sides dearly, especially the Soviets, but it was they, rather than the Germans, who could claim victory in this critical struggle.

LEFT In late October, the Germans had reached Tula, to the south of Moscow. At dawn on 30 October a coordinated final push on the city was launched, but the hastily gathered defenders held their ground in the face of repeated assaults. This proved that the drive on Moscow could be stopped. (Howard Gerrard © Osprey Publishing)

PEARL HARBOR, 7 DECEMBER 1941

The entry of Imperial Japan into World War II was carefully orchestrated and involved simultaneous operations across seven time zones. These initial attacks were designed to inflict the maximum possible damage to the navies of Japan's future enemies, and to pave the way for a series of pre-emptive attacks which would defeat their air and land forces. This done, Japan would be able to create a defensive sphere that stretched from the East Indies to the Central Pacific. The twin centrepieces of this immensely complex plan were the amphibious assault by elements of the Japanese 25th Army on the north-east coast of Malaya, and the large-scale naval air strike on the US Pacific Fleet at its base in Pearl Harbor in Hawaii. The landing in

Malaya would take place early on 8 December, while the Pearl Harbor attack would begin early on 7 December. However, as the two operations took part on opposite sides of the international date line, they would actually start just 30 minutes apart.

Of the two, the Pearl Harbor operation was by far the most ambitious. Until now, no navy had used more than one aircraft carrier in an operation, and a handful of aircraft. Now, the Imperial Japanese Navy would deploy its entre carrier strike force of six aircraft carriers with 465 embarked aircraft. It was a breathtaking display of confidence in this new naval technology, and in the skill of the architects of the operation, Admiral Yamamoto who had conceived the high-risk pre-emptive attack, and Vice Admiral Nagumo who was charged with carrying it out. Nagumo's carrier strike force sailed from Japan on 2 December, under conditions of total secrecy. Nagumo headed east, before turning south on 5 December, timing his progress so he would be within striking range of Hawaii shortly before dawn on 7 December.

Due to a series of intelligence failures, word of the impending attack did not reach Hawaii before it was too late, so the unprovoked Japanese attack came as a complete surprise. The first wave of 183 Japanese aircraft took off at dawn, when the carrier reached their launch point 230 miles north of the Hawaiian island of Oahu. The approaching aircraft were spotted on radar, but the operators assumed they were friendly, and part of a US Navy exercise. At 7.40am the Japanese swept over the northern coast of the island, then split up to attack the main fleet anchorage, as well as the island's airfields. At 7.48am (or 3.18am on 8 December in Japanese time), the first wave began its attack with a mixture of torpedo bombers, dive bombers and level bombers.

They flew off as quickly as they had appeared, but an hour later a second wave of 167 aircraft arrived and resumed the attack. Nagumo cancelled a third strike, so by 9.45am the attack was over. That morning the US Pacific Fleet lost five battleships sunk or beached, and three more damaged. Altogether 2,400 crew and civilians had been killed and many more injured. The Japanese lost 29 aircraft. It was a grievous blow for the US Navy, but importantly their own carriers were at sea, and so crucially they missed the debacle. The Pearl Harbor attack may have been condemned as 'infamy' by America, but in Japan it was viewed as a triumph. The naval value of the attack was limited, though, as the battleships were relatively obsolete by 1941, and the future lay with the aircraft carrier. Their survival would come back to haunt Nagumo the following year.

LEFT One of the first victims of the attack was the battleship USS *Nevada*, which was torpedoed as she tried to make it to the open sea, and was then struck repeatedly by bombs. To prevent his ship from sinking in the main channel, the acting captain decided to beach the *Nevada* at Hospital Point. (Adam Hook © Osprey Publishing)

SINGAPORE, 7 DECEMBER 1941–15 FEBRUARY 1942

As the attack on Pearl Harbor got under way, the Japanese launched a simultaneous assault on Malaya and Singapore, the cornerstone of British power in South Asia. A large invasion force was assembled in the Gulf of Siam and, early on 8 December (7 December in Hawaii), the Japanese landed at six points along the coast of north-eastern Malaya and Siam. A threat to the invasion posed by Force Z – a British battleship and battlecruiser – was removed when they were both sunk by Japanese land-based aircraft. The landings at Singora, Patani and Kota Bahru were

successful, although the latter operation proved costly to the Japanese.

Now that General Yamashita's 25th Army was ashore and supply lines were being established through Siam, the Japanese established a front which spanned the Malay peninsula. They then began their advance south towards Singapore. The British Empire troops facing them – many of them Australian and Indian – lacked the jungle-fighting skills of their opponents. They also lacked the air and tank support enjoyed by the attackers. In a series of encounters at Betong, Machang and Taiping in northern Malaya the defenders were pushed back, retreating south towards Jerantut in the centre of the peninsula, and the Slim River on its western side. The Japanese made good use of captured British airfields, allowing the Japanese air force to gain complete aerial supremacy over the battlefield.

Bombing raids were now carried out on Singapore to disrupt British communications, while after a short pause the Japanese advance down the peninsula was resumed. The Japanese used captured boats to leapfrog the defensive positions on both coasts, and to capture Penang. In early January the British suffered a major defeat at the Slim River, prompting a renewal of the retreat towards Singapore. An Australian victory at Gemas on 14 January failed to stem the tide, as did other rearguard actions further south. By 31 January the remnants of the defenders had withdrawn across the Jahore Bahru causeway into Singapore. Now, Yamashita's three divisions stood on the shore of the Johore Strait, facing the island fortress of Singapore. Unfortunately, these defences faced to seaward rather than to the north. The Japanese were now poised to launch the final blow.

On the night of 8–9 December makeshift assault boats were used to ferry men of the 5th and 18th Japanese Divisions across the strait. Despite losses they were able to establish a bridgehead on the north-west side of Singapore island. Outnumbered, the defending Australian brigade were forced back, as were the troops of another Australian brigade to the east, who faced a similar amphibious assault by the Japanese Imperial Guard Division. The end was now inevitable. The defenders were pushed back to the edge of the city itself, which was being repeatedly bombed by Japanese aircraft, so on 15 December General Percival, commanding the Singapore Garrison, met Yamashita to discuss surrender terms. That evening 130,000 British Empire troops marched into captivity, and Singapore was occupied by the Japanese. It was a humiliating defeat – and one from which the British Empire would never recover.

LEFT During the retreat towards Singapore the British and Commonwealth forces established blocking positions, but the Japanese repeatedly swept these aside. Here, at the Slim River, a column of 30 Japanese tanks backed by infantry tore through the hastily prepared defences of the 11th Indian Division. (Peter Dennis © Osprey Publishing)

MIDWAY, 4 JUNE 1942

Although the Japanese had benefited from their pre-emptive strike at Pearl Harbor they failed to destroy the American carrier fleet. However, it allowed them to expand their defensive perimeter into the South Pacific. This, though, led directly to the Battle of the Coral Sea (28 April–8 May), a clash between the rival carrier forces in the waters to the south of the Solomons. It resulted in the loss of the American carrier *Lexington* and the crippling of another, *Yorktown*, while the Japanese lost the light carrier *Shoho*. In less than a month, though, *Yorktown* was back in service again.

Meanwhile, Vice Admiral Nagumo was planning a much larger operation in the central Pacific. By threatening American-held Midway Island, which was within flying range of Hawaii,

he hoped to entice out the American carriers. Then the larger Japanese carrier strike force would ambush and destroy them. This was part of an even larger operation, codenamed *MI*, which involved landings in the Alaskan Aleutian Islands as well as Midway and neighbouring Kure. Nagumo's carriers would lurk to the north of Midway, waiting to ambush the Americans, while Admiral Yamamoto's main battle fleet would also be at sea in case it was needed. However, what Nagumo didn't realize was that the Americans had broken the Japanese naval signal codes, which meant that they knew what Nagumo was planning. This presented them with the chance to lay their own ambush. In early June Admiral Fletcher's carrier force sailed from Pearl Harbor, and took up position to the north-west of Midway. Rear Admiral Spruance with the carriers *Enterprise* and *Hornet* was joined there by Fletcher in *Yorktown*.

As Yamamoto's fleet set sail, it was assumed the Americans were unaware of their operation until 3 June, when a flying boat sighted the Midway landing force. The following day the Japanese failed to detect the American carriers as Nagumo reached his own position north of Midway. He had four carriers under his command: *Akagi*, *Kaga*, *Hiryu* and *Soryu*. That morning he ordered their aircraft to bombard Midway. But they had already been detected, and a land-based strike was launched from Midway to attack them. This was driven off with heavy losses, just as the Japanese strike was returning. At that moment Nagumo's scout planes spotted American ships to the north, which included one carrier.

The cautious approach would have been to rearm his planes with torpedoes rather than bombs, and attack the carrier. Instead, Nagumo ordered a second strike on Midway. At 9.30am, torpedo bombers from *Enterprise* and *Yorktown* attacked the Japanese carriers just as their flight decks were filled with aircraft rearming and refuelling. The protective ring of Japanese fighters intercepted them, though, and most were shot down. However, this distracted the Japanese fighters and they didn't detect the approach of a second strike of American dive bombers. Nagumo's flagship *Akagi* was hit, along with *Kaga* and *Soryu*.

The remaining carrier *Hiryu* launched her aircraft and followed the departing Americans, who led them to *Yorktown*, which was damaged and was later sunk by a submarine as she limped home. Meanwhile a third American strike crippled *Hiryu* that evening as the Japanese fleets withdrew. The loss of four carriers was a blow from which the Japanese never recovered. Midway was a decisive American victory, and it was achieved entirely by naval aircraft.

LEFT The last of the Japanese carriers to be attacked off Midway was the *Hiryu*. Captain Kaku tried to evade the bombs of these Dauntless dive-bombers from *Enterprise* and *Yorktown*, but four 1,000-pound bombs hit the forward part of her flight deck, and the carrier was crippled and set ablaze. (Howard Gerrard © Osprey Publishing)

EL ALAMEIN, 15 JULY–AUGUST–SEPTEMBER 1942

In February 1941 the British regarded their campaign in the Western Desert as a thorough success. The Italians had been comprehensively defeated and pushed back 500 miles. Then, within a month, everything changed. The arrival of General Rommel and his German Afrika Korps rejuvenated the Italians, and in late March Rommel's counter-offensive drove the British back to the Egyptian border. For more than a year, the tide of war ebbed and flowed as first the British drove the Germans back, and then Rommel counter-attacked. By late June 1942, though, Rommel's army had advanced deep into Egypt, until he was less than 200 miles from Cairo. The British Eighth Army now held a defensive line a little to the east of Rommel, near

the coastal railway halt of El Alamein. It seemed that if Rommel could make one more push, then he could secure control of both Egypt and the Suez Canal.

The key to the British position was Ruweisat Ridge, ten miles south of the coast, and another smaller ridge, Alam Halfa, seven miles to the south-east of the ridge. The front was fortified using minefields and wire, and the British troops dug in behind them. After probing these defences, Rommel held back to bring up supplies before launching an all-out attack. In fact it was General Auchinleck, commanding the Eighth Army, who began the fight there in mid-July. The battle for Ruweisat Ridge and other key points continued for a week, but neither side managed to deal the enemy a decisive blow, so the battle ended in a stalemate that left both sides battered and exhausted. Although Auchinleck had held Rommel, Churchill still replaced him with General Montgomery. Now it would be 'Monty', a cautious commander, who would have to take the fight to Rommel.

He was helped by Ultra, top level intelligence from broken German codes, and was forewarned of Rommel's intentions. Montgomery was able to halt a limited offensive by Rommel launched against Alam Halfa on 31 August. It petered out in the face of British air attacks, artillery bombardment and well-dug-in defenders on the ridge itself and Rommel withdrew to his original lines on 2 September. For the next seven weeks Montgomery reinforced his army and prepared it for the offensive that lay ahead. By now he had a marked advantage in men, tanks and guns. Late on 23 October the Eighth Army's assault was preceded by a mass bombardment.

The attack the next day was a slow affair, as the British had to clear paths through the minefields. The most heavily contested advance was along the coast, where the British and Australians were forced to hold off a major counter-attack by Rommel's 21st Panzer Division. The battle developed into a series of bitterly contested fights for key battlefield features, such as control of the coastal road and nearby Kidney Hill. Frequent Axis counter-attacks wore down Rommel's tank force, while Montgomery kept the bulk of his armour in reserve. Then, on 2 November, the British broke through the front between Kidney Hill and the coast, and Montgomery unleashed his armour. Rommel's last counter-attack was brushed aside, and on 4 November he gave the order to withdraw back to Libya. In fact, the retreat would continue all the way into Tunisia, 1,500 miles to the east. The Battle of El Alamein was the turning point of the War in the Desert, and an immense tonic to the Allied cause.

LEFT At El Alamein, Rommel's last real chance to defeat Montgomery's 8th Army came on 1 September. He counter-attacked with the 15th and 21st Panzer Divisions, assaulting Alam Halfa Ridge, but the panzers were eventually forced to retreat in the face of heavy artillery and anti-tank gun fire. (Howard Gerrard © Osprey Publishing)

GUADALCANAL, 7 AUGUST 1942–8 FEBRUARY 1943

After Pearl Harbor the Japanese advanced rapidly throughout the South Pacific to create a defensive perimeter. In the south-west Pacific this incorporated the Solomon Islands. In May this perimeter was expanded down the Solomons chain to reach the small island of Tulagi and the larger island of Guadalcanal to the south. Work then began establishing a forward air base near Guadalcanal's Lunga Point. For the Allies, this represented a direct threat to the vital sea route between Australia and the United States; therefore, plans were laid to attack these two

forward Japanese bases, and so remove the threat to Allied shipping.

On 7 August the 1st US Marine Division led by Major General Vandergrift launched a combined amphibious assault on Tulagi and Guadalcanal. Tulagi and neighbouring Gavutu-Tanambogo were captured after two days of bitter fighting, while on Guadalcanal the airfield was quickly overrun and a beachhead established. The Japanese were quick to react, and a naval task force was sent to attack the Allied fleet assembled off the northern coast of the island. In a night attack off Savo Island the Japanese sank four American and one Australian cruisers, but failed to destroy the American transport ships. So, the build-up continued, despite regular naval bombardment and air attacks. The airfield, renamed Henderson Field, was made operational, and its fighters did what they could to protect the fragile bridgehead.

The Japanese also sent troops, landed to the west of the bridgehead by nightly destroyer shuttles nicknamed 'The Tokyo Express'. The first of these, the Ichiki Detachment, arrived on 16 August and five days later it assaulted the western side of the American perimeter near the Tenaru River. The Japanese force was virtually wiped out in this frontal assault but this set the pattern for a string of further clashes as Japanese reinforcements were hurled piecemeal against the American perimeter. Over two weeks in late August the Marines repulsed similar assaults along the Tenaru, before the Japanese switched their attention to a key jungle-clad ridge to the south of Henderson Field. It was named Edson's Ridge after the colonel who commanded the Marine Raiders who held it.

On 12 September the Japanese launched a series of all-out assaults on the ridge, with a 3,000-strong brigade of veteran troops. The decisive attack came on the night of 12–13 September, when the heavily outnumbered Marines were forced out of their front-line positions on Hill 80 by a bayonet charge, but held Hill 123 behind it, while other Marine detachments stopped Japanese attempts to encircle the ridge. By the afternoon of 13 September it was over, as the remaining Japanese withdrew. The battle for 'Bloody Ridge' was a turning point of the battle. Other assaults would follow in October and November, but the Americans were now in firm control of the island. On 8 February the last of the Japanese troops on Guadalcanal were withdrawn, leaving the remains of over 20,000 of their comrades behind them. American losses were just over 1,750. With the capture of Guadalcanal the Allies gained the initiative in the Pacific, and would retain it as they continued their long and bloody drive towards Japan.

LEFT During September the Japanese launched a series of attacks against the 1st Marine Division dug in along the Matikanu River, to the west of the American bridgehead. Despite the bravery shown by the Japanese, these unsupported and improvised assaults were all repulsed with heavy losses. (Steve Noon © Osprey Publishing)

STALINGRAD, 19 AUGUST 1942–2 FEBRUARY 1943

For much of the winter of 1941–42 the Axis troops on the Eastern Front remained on the defensive along a 1,000-mile front line. The Soviets launched a series of counter-attacks though, which achieved some success. The Germans contained these, but also conserved their strength in preparation for their summer offensive, codenamed *Fall Blau* (Case Blue). Its primary objective was the capture of the oil fields in the Caucasus, and the destruction of Soviet resistance west of the River Volga. *Fall Blau* began on 19 June.

The German advance was relatively swift, and by 6 July General Bock's Army Group South had reached the River Don near Voronezh. At that point the panzers turned south, clearing the bend of the Don that lay between Milerovo and Kalach. Soviet reinforcements managed to hold the line of the Don to the north, but were unable to stop the Germans from bridging the river near Kalach, and then driving towards Stalingrad on the Volga, just 40 miles to the east. Stalingrad (formerly Tsaritsyn and now Volgograd) was of great strategic importance due to its location on the upper Volga, while its name gave it a huge symbolic import too. By 19 August, General von Paulus' 6th Army had reached the western outskirts of the sprawling 30-mile-long city. He began his attack immediately, his assault columns supported by massed artillery and bombers.

Defending Stalingrad were elements of General Lopatin's already battered 62nd and 64th Armies. Within four days Paulus had reached the Volga in the north of the city, and further south his men advanced block by block to push the defenders back towards the river. On 7 September, when Lopatin ordered a withdrawal he was sacked by Stalin and replaced by the more stoic General Chuikov. A week later, supported by an immense artillery barrage, Paulus launched a major attack and reached the Volga in the southern portion of the city, and isolated Soviet outposts elsewhere. The fighting now centred around these outposts: the Tractor Factory in the north, the Red October Factory in the south, and then Central Station, 'Pavlov's House' and the grain elevators further south. In the centre the high ground of the Mamayev Kurgan where Chuikov had his headquarters was subjected to a relentless series of assaults.

The courage shown by the Soviet defenders of these last strongholds was exceptional. Fighting often degenerated into hand-to-hand combat over the ruins, fought with knives and bayonets. Attack and counter-attack were commonplace – the ruins of the Central Station changed hands 15 times during the battle. Somehow, though, the defenders held on, supported by a trickle of reinforcements and supplies from across the Volga. Then, on 19 November, everything changed. The Soviets had been husbanding their troops, and now launched Operation *Uranus*, a major offensive to the north and south of Stalingrad. On 23 November these pincers united near Kalach, trapping the 6th Army in Stalingrad. A powerful German relief attempt failed, and despite the flying in of supplies Paulus and his 6th Army was trapped. They fought on, but the situation was hopeless, and on 31 January Paulus surrendered together with 91,000 of his men. Stalingrad was arguably the most decisive battle of the war.

LEFT The brutal struggle for the city often involved fighting for control of the ruins of key buildings. One of these was 'The Commissar's House', the strongly built administration building of the Barrikady Factory. The Germans finally stormed and captured it on 13 November, after a costly assault. (Steve Noon © Osprey Publishing)

KHARKOV, 19 FEBRUARY–15 MARCH 1943

After the Battle of Stalingrad, the Soviets pursued the retreating Germans into Ukraine. On General Golikov's Veronezh Front and General Vatutin's South-West Front the line of the River Don was reached, and then crossed. Field Marshal von Manstein's outnumbered Army Group Don was at risk of being encircled between the Don and the River Donetz to the west, but Manstein secured Hitler's reluctant permission to form a more secure line along the west bank of the Donetz. The Soviet advance continued, though, and both Kursk and Belgorod were retaken. On 16 February Kharkov fell when the SS Panzer Corps defending the city withdrew to avoid encirclement. This also left a 100-mile gap in the front between Army Group

Centre in the north and Manstein's command, which had been renamed Army Group South. It was a potentially catastrophic situation for the Germans, as Golikov and Vatutin now stood poised to either encircle Manstein or push west across Ukraine.

For Manstein this crisis also brought opportunity as he realized that the Soviets had over-extended themselves and were fast running out of fuel. Both armies were exhausted and under-strength, but Manstein still had a powerful reserve at his disposal. I and IV Panzer Corps were to the south of this gap in the front, which the Soviets were now streaming into. General Hausser, the new commander of the SS Panzer Corps, was capable of holding the line to the north-west of Kharkov. This would slow the Soviet advance, buying time for Manstein to launch his counter-stroke. It began on 19 February as I Panzer Corps drove north from Stalino towards Izyum while IV Panzer Korps also advanced on Izyum from Dniepropetrovsk, on the south-west side of the Soviet salient. The 4th Air Fleet provided close air support and ensured control of the skies during the operation.

Within a week the Soviets had been driven back over 60 miles, although this wasn't about just reclaiming territory. On reaching the frozen Donetz near Izyum the two panzer corps turned north towards Kharkov, to encircle the best part of two Soviet armies. By 4 March, Manstein's panzers were grouped around Krasnograd, 50 miles south-west of Kharkov. The following day Manstein unleashed them in a drive to encircle the city, supported by Hausser's SS troops and VII Panzer Corps from Army Group Centre, and XLVIII Panzer Corps, which had just joined Manstein's command. The encirclement went smoothly and was achieved by 12 March.

Rather than take part in the encirclement battle Hausser's three SS panzer divisions advanced directly into Kharkov and smashed their way through the city's defences, and the city fell on 14 March. That left Manstein's other troops to consolidate their gains around Kharkov, and press on to capture Bielgorod, 45 miles to the north-east. In just four weeks Manstein had not only plugged the gap in the front but had inflicted a major blow on the enemy. This bought the time the Germans desperately needed to rest and regroup after Stalingrad, and to prepare their armies for an even greater offensive at Kursk in summer 1943.

LEFT The Germans were quick to react to the new Soviet threat around Kharkov, and their assault on 20 February took the enemy unawares, encircling four tank corps. Here, troops of the 7th Panzer Division are show moving in to seal off the 'Kessel' or pocket near the village of Krasnoarmeyskoye. (Adam Hook © Osprey Publishing)

KURSK, 4 JULY–27 AUGUST 1943

The Soviet advances in late 1942 and early 1943 and Manstein's counter-offensive at Kharkov that followed paved the way for the great Battle of Kursk. Between them they refashioned the otherwise largely static front line. By the end of March a large bulge around the city of Kursk protruded for 60 miles into the German line between Orel and Kharkov. Field Marshal von Manstein, commanding Army Group South, was convinced that after rebuilding his army he should go back onto the offensive and cut off this bulge at its base. This would then trap the hundreds of thousands of Soviet troops inside it, avenge Stalingrad, and end the deadlock on the Eastern Front. The German High Command remained unconvinced, and the offensive,

codenamed Operation *Citadel*, was delayed until early July, in order to buy time for the Germans to rebuild their forces. This also gave the Soviets time to dig in.

For *Citadel* the Germans assembled 750,000 men, almost 2,500 tanks, assault guns and tank destroyers, 7,400 guns and 1,800 aircraft. This represented roughly two-thirds of the German tanks and aircraft on the entire Eastern Front. Manstein's plan called for a drive north by Army Group South to link up with a matching drive south by Field Marshal Kluge's Army Group Centre. Both pincers would be spearheaded by a panzer army made up of four panzer corps. For their part the Soviets had prepared a defence in depth, protected by minefields and fortified positions, and supported by anti-tank guns, artillery and tanks. The southern side of the salient was defended by General Vatutin's Voronezh Front, while General Rokissovski's Centre Front protected the northern side of the bulge. In reserve to the east was General Koniev's Steppe Front.

The great assault began at dawn on 5 July. General Model's IX Panzer Army and General Hoth's IV Panzer Army led the advance in the north and south respectively. However, the defences proved hard to penetrate and it took Hoth a week to advance 20 miles. In the north, Kluge, supported by General Model's IX Panzer Army, only advanced eight miles before being halted at Ponyri Station, on the Soviets' third defensive line. Effectively, both pincers had now stalled. The Germans had suffered heavy tank losses, including many of their new Tiger and Panther tanks, and so Hoth and Model paused to regroup. It was at that crucial point that the Soviets unleashed their own tank reserves from Koniev's front.

Early on 12 July General Rotmistrov's 5th Guard Tank Army advanced on Hoth near the little town of Prokhorovka. II SS Panzer Corps advanced to meet them and a swirling tank battle followed which, though spectacular, ended in stalemate. Manstein's southern pincer had been stopped as thoroughly as Kluge's northern one. Hitler ordered the operation to be cancelled. Then, on 2 August, the Soviets launched a pair of offensives of their own. In the north Kluge was driven back over 80 miles by General Popov's Bryansk Front, and Orel was liberated. In the south, Koniev and Vatutin did the same to Manstein, and recaptured Kharkov. Operation *Citadel* was the last large-scale German offensive in the east, and instead of avenging Stalingrad as Manstein had hoped, it paved the way for a relentless Soviet drive on Berlin.

LEFT On 12 July, Pavel Rotmistrov's 5th Guard Tank Army counter-attacked the German panzer divisions at the tip of the southern salient near the village of Prokhorovka. In the close-range battle that followed both sides lost hundreds of tanks, but the Germans were eventually forced to pull back. (Graham Turner © Osprey Publishing)

IMPHAL AND KOHIMA, MARCH–JULY 1944

Following the Japanese capture of Singapore in February 1942, the Japanese 15th Army advanced into British-held Burma. Their objective was to sever the supply line of the Chinese nationalists, and to strengthen their hold on south-east Asia. The capture of Mandalay and Rangoon secured control of this rugged country, and by the summer all of Burma was under Japanese control. For the moment, though, there was no will to continue the fight into British India. Instead, the region remained relatively quiet until late 1942, when the Americans decided to support the Chinese. This required the re-establishment of a supply route through Burma. The British reluctantly agreed to do what they could, but their first tentative

offensive in the Arakan region of south-western Burma ended in failure.

However, the more successful operation by Brigadier Wingate's Chindits in central Burma in early 1943 led the Japanese to realize the threat posed by further British-led operations in the region. Then, in October, American and Chinese raiders advancing from China raided into Northern Burma so Lieutenant-General Mutaguchi, commanding the 85,000-strong 15th Army, was ordered to launch a pre-emptive invasion across the border into British India, to curtail further raids and to end any chance of re-establishing a supply route to China. This offensive, codenamed Operation *U-Go*, began in February 1944. A diversionary attack was made in the Arakan, which sucked in six divisions of the British Indian Army.

In early March Mutaguchi advanced across the Indian border. Forewarned of the attack, Lieutenant-General Slim planned to withdraw the bulk of his troops to the Imphal plain, where they could be easily supplied and supported by air, artillery and armour. Rearguard actions in the Manipur Valley and the Samra Hills slowed the Japanese advance, giving Slim time to airlift in reinforcements from Arakan. In early April,

though, the Japanese 31st Division reached the fortified outpost of Kohima, 80 miles north of Imphal. For 12 days the battalion-sized Indian Army garrison repulsed a series of ferocious Japanese attacks, and on 18 April the outpost was relieved. The Japanese division withdrew, just as Mutaguchi's southern pincers were closing in on Imphal.

Here Lieutenant-General Scoones' IV Corps were dug in around the town, and from late March the Japanese launched a series of attacks on Imphal's perimeter. The Japanese made little headway, though, and although casualties mounted steadily on both sides, the Indian Army was able to resupply and reinforce its troops, while the Japanese could not. Mutaguchi continued these assaults long after it was clear his chance of victory had slipped away. Finally, on 22 June, fresh Indian Army troops advanced on Imphal from the direction of Kohima, and the Japanese finally began to withdraw. Slim then launched his troops in a counter-attack, capturing the village of Ukhrul to block the Japanese retreat. As a result, when the remnants of the 15th Army finally crossed the Chindwin River to safety, it had lost two-thirds of its strength. Imphal and Kohima proved to be the decisive battle in the Burmese theatre. Not only was India saved, but the supply route to China could now be opened. It also paved the way for the Allied conquest of Burma.

LEFT At Kohima in mid-April the two sides faced each other across what had recently been a pristine tennis court, next to the British deputy commissioner's bungalow. The Japanese launched repeated assaults across this open space, but the men of the Royal West Kents held on despite heavy losses. (Peter Dennis © Osprey Publishing)

SAINT-LÔ, 25–31 JULY 1944

On D-Day, 6 June 1944, the Allied armies landed in Normandy. The immense amphibious invasion was a success and casualties were lighter than expected, despite the strong resistance experienced at Omaha Beach in the American sector. Once ashore, the next task was to consolidate and expand the bridgehead. Over the weeks that followed, the Allies advanced in the face of growing German resistance. To the east of the bridgehead the city of Caen remained in German hands, but further west, on the Cherbourg peninsula, American troops had reached the outer defences of Cherbourg itself. In the centre, the British were held up in the face of a large concentration of German panzer formations, but on their right flank, the Americans fought their

way through the difficult *bocage* country to capture the town of Saint-Lô, where roads radiated out across southern Normandy.

To win the campaign, the Allies needed somehow to break the deadlock in Normandy and find a way to break through the German defences. General Montgomery, commanding the British and Canadians, had launched a string of small-scale offensives in his eastern sector, but while these had pushed the Germans back, they had failed to breach their defences. However, these did attract the bulk of the German panzer forces and tie them down. This meant that in the relatively quieter American sector to the west, the German defences had been stripped of most of their best formations and their reserves. General Bradley, commanding the First US Army, realized this, and had assembled a powerful reserve. On 25 July, in a major offensive codenamed Operation *Cobra*, Bradley unleashed these fresh troops against General Hausser's weak German 7th Army.

Bradley's initial plan called for a limited advance south-west of Saint-Lô, to serve as a jumping-off point for the main offensive. It was preceded on 24 July by a mass carpet bombing by 835 American bombers east of Saint-Lô. This

was repeated with over double the aircraft the following morning. Their bombs shattered Hausser's best formation, the Panzer Lehr Division, but caused American casualties too. Nevertheless, the ground assault by the US VII Corps followed the bombing and, despite some pockets of resistance, the dazed German defenders were overwhelmed. By nightfall Major-General Collins' VII Corps had advanced up to six miles. The attack was resumed by fresh American troops the following morning, supported by waves of American fighter-bombers. In three days the German resistance had crumbled, and Bradley's armoured divisions were pushing on to the south.

At this point Bradley launched a general advance and threw in his reserves. On 28 June the key junction town of Coutances was captured, cutting off the bulk of General von Choltitz's LXXXIV Corps, deployed further north. Hausser ordered it to break out, but most of it was destroyed by American air and ground units. There were no effective German reserves, and over the next three days the Americans advanced rapidly, on 31 July capturing Avrances, the gateway to Brittany. Field Marshal von Kluge, the senior German commander in Normandy, tried to support Hausser by assembling a panzer reserve, but by then it was too late. The breakout had been achieved and now, as Bradley assumed command of 12 Army Group, a new force, General Patton's Third US Army, joined the fight. A month later Kluge's army group would be destroyed and the Allies would liberate Paris.

LEFT The sector of Normandy selected for Operation *Cobra* was hardly ideal for major breakthrough, as it was 'bocage country', where fields were divided by high-banked hedges, ideally suited for defence. Here, though, American GIs are shown fighting their way through these defended natural obstacles. (Johnny Shumate © Osprey Publishing)

LEYTE GULF, 22–27 OCTOBER 1944

Despite defeats at Guadalcanal and Papua New Guinea, the Japanese defensive perimeter in the Pacific remained largely intact for much of 1943. That autumn, though, the Americans began a series of amphibious attacks which would rip this perimeter apart. The capture of Tarawa, Makin and Kwajalein in the Gilbert and Marshall Islands breached the perimeter and gave the Allies access to the Marianas chain. Between June and September, the Japanese-held islands of Saipan, Tinian, Guam and Palau were captured, albeit at a huge cost.

That June the Japanese Navy suffered a major defeat in the Battle of the Philippine Sea. This American victory, won by carrier-based aircraft, forced the Japanese to abandon their main base

at Truk and to pull their fleet back to Singapore. It also left the Western Pacific open to American attack. It was decided to retake the Philippines, with initial landings at Leyte scheduled for 20 October. For their part the Japanese planned to use their fleet to fight a 'decisive battle' wherever the Americans attacked, so when it became clear Leyte was the target, the Japanese gathered their three task forces and sent them towards the Philippines. What followed would be the biggest naval battle of the war.

Admiral Ozawa's Northern Force, which included four carriers, would draw the bulk of Admiral Halsey's US Third Fleet away from Leyte. Then, Admirals Kurita and Nishimura, commanding the Centre and Southern Forces made up of surface warships, would launch a pincer attack around Leyte to attack the invasion fleet. Their approach to the Philippines was detected by American submarines, so when Kurita's Centre Force passed through the Sibuyan Sea in the centre of the Philippine archipelago, it was harried by air strikes from Halsey's Fast Carrier Force, commanded by Vice Admiral Mitscher. On the night of 24–25 June, as Nishimura's smaller Southern Force passed through the Surigao Strait south of Leyte, it

came under attack from American torpedo boats. Then shortly before 4am, Nishimura encountered Rear Admiral Oldendorf's powerful task group of cruisers and battleships, deployed in line across its path. In what was the last battleship duel in history, these sank Nishimura's flagship, the battleship *Yamashiro*, and the battleship *Fuso*. The rest of the Japanese fleet withdrew.

Later that morning Kurita's force was attacked off the Philippine island of Samar. Three escort carrier groups of Vice Admiral Kinkaid's Seventh Fleet launched a series of air strikes. One carrier group, though, was unlucky enough to come within gun range of the Japanese. It was fired on by four Japanese battleships before it could withdraw, and the escort carrier *Gambier Bay* was sunk. Lacking carriers, Kurita was supported by land-based aircraft, some of which launched 'kamikaze' attacks on the American carriers – the first kamikaze missions of the war, which sank the carrier *St. Lo*. Having lost the battleship *Musashi*, and with his other battleships damaged, Kurita decided to withdraw. Finally, that same morning Ozawa's Northern Force clashed with the American Fast Carrier Force, and in a series of devastating air strikes the Japanese lost the carrier *Zuikaku* and two light carriers. With that Ozawa withdrew, ending the last serious attempt by the Japanese Navy to turn the tide of war in the Pacific.

LEFT On the morning of 24 October Admiral Kurita's Central Force in the Sibuyan Sea came under attack from aircraft operating from the carriers of Admiral Kincaid's Seventh Fleet. During the day the powerful battleship *Musashi* was hit by up to 15 torpedoes and she finally sank that evening. (Jim Laurier © Osprey Publishing)

HIROSHIMA AND NAGASAKI, 6–9 AUGUST 1945

By the start of 1945 the US Navy dominated the Western Pacific, but the Japanese homeland still lay out of reach of American land-based aircraft. Consequently, the Americans needed to capture islands which could serve as air bases within bomber range of the Japanese mainland, so the US Joint Chiefs of Staff approved assaults on the islands of Iwo Jima and Okinawa. Iwo Jima was captured in March, after a hard-fought five-week-long battle and at the cost of 6,000 American lives. The invasion of Okinawa began on 26 March, and it would take just over three

months to totally clear the Japanese from this island fortress. This cost the lives of 14,000 American troops. High though the cost was, this now gave the Americans bases from which to launch bomber raids on Japan. Long-range B-29 'Superfortress' bombers could also operate from Saipan, Guam and Tinian. Large-scale low-level bombing raids were launched from these island bases, targeting Japanese cities. These produced fire storms that caused widespread devastation and loss of life. The American hope for the bombing campaign was that this would force the Japanese to surrender, without necessitating an Allied assault on Japan itself. Given the fanatical resistance the Japanese had shown, planners expected extremely high casualties if the Allied invasion of Japan went ahead. However, as a surrender looked unlikely, the US Government began considering another option, a weapon that could well end the war at a single stroke.

From 1942 on, a team of American scientists had been working on just such a weapon. This team worked in extreme secrecy at a research facility at Los Alamos in New Mexico. Their aim was the development of a nuclear weapon, an air-dropped bomb which derived its destructive power from initiating a nuclear reaction, which produced a nuclear explosion. Finally, in July 1945, the first bomb was successfully tested in New Mexico. Just over a week later, after Allied peace terms were rejected, President Truman authorized the use of this weapon against Japan. By then Hiroshima and Nagasaki had been chosen as the primary and secondary targets.

Early on 6 August three B-29 bombers of the 393rd Bombardment Squadron left Tinian and flew north towards Japan. *Enola Gay* carried the atomic payload, while the other two B-29s were there to film the detonation and to record its effects. It took six hours to reach the target, and the 'Little Boy' bomb was released at 8.15am. The detonation flattened everything within a one-mile radius and the resulting firestorm caused further destruction. The mission had been a success, but the hoped-for Japanese surrender never came, so a second mission was authorized. At 11.02am on 9 August the 'Fat Man' atomic bomb exploded over Nagasaki, dropped by another B-29 named *Bockscar*. This had the desired effect. The following morning the Japanese emperor agreed to surrender. Although as many as 200,000 Japanese people would die from the blast or from radiation, the cost was considered low, compared to the potential casualties on both sides that would have resulted from an Allied invasion of Japan. The war was over, and the world had entered a new and terrifying nuclear age.

LEFT At 8.15am on 15 August, the B-29 bomber 'Enola Gay' released its single bomb payload. The 'Little Boy' uranium-powered atomic bomb detonated over central Hiroshima less than a minute later. A shockwave immediately radiated out from 'ground zero', marked by a spreading mushroom cloud. (John White © Osprey Publishing)

THE MODERN AGE

INCHON, 10–19 SEPTEMBER 1950

The end of World War II saw the emergence of two superpowers, the United States and the Soviet Union. Postwar harmony was short-lived, as tensions rose following the consolidation of Soviet control over Eastern Europe and the division of Germany. Another potential flashpoint was Korea, which had been annexed by Japan in 1910. At the end of the war the Soviets occupied the northern portion of Korea, while the Americans occupied the country south of the 38th Parallel. By 1948, through diplomatic agreement, the country had become partitioned into two zones. Although the occupying troops left in 1948–49, North and South Korea retained the political systems of their former occupiers. Tension between the two Korean states increased

amid border clashes and Communist-inspired insurrections. Soviet and Chinese advisers armed and trained the North Korean People's Army (KPA), and in June 1950 the country's leader Kim Il-Sung approved its use in an invasion of South Korea.

This began at dawn on 25 June. The Republic of Korea (ROK) army was poorly equipped and outnumbered. It was forced to give ground, and three days later the South Korean capital of Seoul fell to the North Koreans. By 30 June the situation had become desperate, as the ROK army was now reduced to a fraction of its pre-war strength, and troops and refugees alike fled south, away from the advancing KPA. On 27 June, following the United Nations' condemnation of the invasion, President Truman decided to intervene as part of a UN coalition to support South Korea. Two days later the US 24th Infantry Division was airlifted to Korea from Japan, but was unable to stop the KPA advance in a string of holding actions, and withdrew towards Pusan on the southern coast of Korea.

There, General MacArthur planned to establish a 140-mile-long defensive perimeter, where his ROK, US and UN troops could hold off the attackers. For the next six weeks the KPA hurled itself at the Pusan Perimeter, but the line held. Gradually, it became clear that the invaders had been pushed to their limits and were short of men and supplies. By early September MacArthur had the resources to strike back. To relieve the perimeter, he planned to bypass the KPA, and instead land a powerful force 200 miles to the north, at Inchon near Seoul.

Air attacks on Inchon began on 10 September, and three days later a powerful American-led UN naval task force bombarded shore positions in the area. Then, at dawn on 15 September, the US Marines landed on Green Beach on the east side of Inchon. That afternoon, more landings were made on Red and Blue Beaches and by nightfall the outnumbered KPA had been driven back from the beachheads. The following day, the 5th Marine Division and 7th Infantry Division pressed on into Inchon itself, to secure control of the port. Over the next three days the last pockets of resistance were cleared, and the Americans pressed on towards Seoul. The fighting there would continue, but meanwhile more US and ROK troops flooded ashore to spearhead the offensive inland. The result was a hasty KPA retreat from Pusan before they were cut off. Inchon has been described as the most successful US-led military operation since World War II, and although the Korean War would continue, it remains MacArthur's finest hour.

LEFT Although the initial UN landings around Inch'on were largely unopposed, resistance strengthened as the attackers pressed on towards the South Korean capital of Seoul. On 26 September the US 7th Marines were pinned down by heavy fire to the north-west of the city, until reinforcements arrived. (Peter Dennis © Osprey Publishing)

DIEN BIEN PHU, 13 MARCH–7 MAY 1954

During World War II, the colony of French Indochina (now Vietnam) was occupied by the Japanese. Then, in August 1945, the French reclaimed the southern portion of the country south of the latitude of 16° North, while in the north a Vietnamese republic was proclaimed, led by its Communist president, Ho Chi Minh. The French advanced north and quickly established control of Hanoi and other towns in the north, and so assumed de facto control of the whole of Vietnam. Ho Chi Minh and his supporters fought back, though, and a low-level guerrilla war ensued. This struggle became known as the First Indochina War. By 1949 the armed Communist insurgents, known as the Viet Minh, were receiving military aid directly from

China. The war then took on a more conventional aspect, as regularly organized Viet Minh troops attacked French bases, supply lines and outposts.

With American support the war simmered on into the 1950s. By 1953, however, the Communist insurgents controlled much of northern Indochina, outside the fortified Lattre Line set up to protect Hanoi and the Red River Delta. The military situation had become a stalemate, as General Giap, Ho Chi Minh's senior commander, lacked the resources to attack the Lattre Line, while the French lacked the manpower to reclaim the countryside. It was then that the French commander in Indochina, General Navarre, evolved a plan, codenamed Operation *Castor*, designed to bring the Viet Minh to battle on favourable terms.

Navarre planned to entice the Viet Minh out by establishing a fortified camp at Dien Bien Phu in the highlands of Tonkin. The Viet Minh had been operating in nearby Laos, and if encouraged to attack the camp, they would fall prey to coordinated French fire. Therefore, on 20 November, French paratroops were dropped on Dien Bien Phu, led by Colonel de Castries and began digging. The main fortified camp was surrounded by seven satellite positions, all of which were given women's names. The 10,000 defenders, who were a mix of French paratroop, Foreign Legion, Colonial and local units, waited for the enemy.

Meanwhile Giap had gathered his forces and occupied the surrounding jungle-clad hills. By March he had three Viet Minh divisions, a total of almost 50,000 men, supported by artillery. On 13 March Giap bombarded the defences, and then his men assaulted and captured the French outpost of Béatrice. The following day the Viet Minh stormed Gabrielle and repulsed a French counter-attack. This prompted the Vietnamese defenders of another, Anne-Marie, to defect. Both sides then paused to regroup, although the bombardment continued. When the attacks resumed on 30 March the Viet Minh assaulted the centre of the French defences. This turned into a bitter struggle that lasted for days before the attackers withdrew.

For the next month, Giap besieged the French, and prepared for a series of major assaults. When they came on 1 May, three outposts were overrun. Five days later a second massed assault captured Elaine, another key satellite, then on 7 May the Viet Minh finally overran the French central position and with it de Castries' headquarters. Over 11,000 French troops were captured, just in time for Ho Chi Minh to announce the victory at the Geneva Peace Talks. This led directly to the French withdrawal from Indochina two years later.

LEFT After three weeks of enduring heavy fire, the defenders of strongpoint Elaine-1 were attacked in the evening of 1 May. Waves of attackers from two veteran Viet Minh regiments pressed the French paratroopers, and eventually at 2am the garrison's survivors withdrew to a nearby fort, Elaine-4. (Peter Dennis © Osprey Publishing)

THE GOLAN HEIGHTS, 5–10 JUNE 1967

Since the establishment of the State of Israel in May 1948, its relations with the surrounding Arab countries had been extremely hostile. Although the Arab-Israeli War of 1948–49 secured Israel's borders, tensions remained high, particularly in 1956 when Israel invaded Egypt in support of the Anglo-French attack on Port Said. For many Israelis the threat posed by the belligerency of their neighbours never went away, particularly in Galilee, overlooked by the Syrian-held Golan Heights. There, Israeli kibbutz settlements were regularly targeted by Syrian guns. In early June 1967, Egypt's President Nasser blockaded the Straits of Tiran, denying access to Israel's southern port of Eilat. As Egyptian troops mobilized around Gaza and the

Sinai Peninsula, it was clear that war was imminent.

On 5 June, as Syria and Jordan joined the mobilization, the Israelis launched pre-emptive airstrikes against Egyptian airfields, effectively destroying the Egyptian Air Force. This marked the start of the Six Day War. At first, the Israelis were able to concentrate on the campaigns against Egypt and Jordan. Nevertheless, Syrian airstrikes were launched which prompted an Israeli attack on Syrian airfields destroying 57 aircraft. Then, on 6 June, the Syrians attacked Tel Dan, just below the Golan Heights. The attack was repulsed, but it raised the spectre of war erupting on another front. However, Israeli victories in the Sinai and West Bank permitted reinforcements to be sent north into Galilee, and General Elazar of Israel's Northern Command was ordered to go over onto the offensive.

The Syrians had nine infantry brigades on the Golan Heights supported by tanks and artillery. Elazar had seven brigades, including armoured and mechanized formations, and was forced to attack uphill against a larger and well-entrenched army. Nevertheless, the assault began on 9 June, with the 8th Armoured Brigade's advance in the north near Kfar Szold supported by engineers to clear mines and wire from their path. The attackers suffered heavy losses in men and tanks, but eventually the Syrians were pushed back, giving the Israelis a foothold on the Heights. Further north the Golani and 45th Brigades scaled the Heights to capture the stronghold at Dardara, then pressed on to secure Banias. This too was a hard-fought and costly operation. In the centre the 37th Armoured Brigade gained the high ground, then penetrated the Syrian defences as far as Rawiya. More assaults on either side of the Sea of Galilee also gained a foothold on the Heights.

With the border defences captured, the Israelis spent the night of 9–10 June pressing on, to expand their Golan bridgehead. At dawn a pincer attack on the Syrians in the northern Golan revealed the enemy had retreated, and so the three Israeli brigades attacked the key town of Kuneitra, as well as Mount Hermon. Advances further south were equally spectacular, as Israeli columns drove through the now disorganized Syrian formations, and advanced on the Syrian supply centre of Butmiya, over 30 miles to the east. That afternoon a ceasefire was agreed, and the fighting stopped. By then, however, the Golan Heights were firmly in Israeli hands and so the safety of Galilee was secured.

LEFT While advancing on Janin in the West Bank, the Israeli 45th Armoured Brigade encountered heavy resistance and had to fight a major tank battle with Jordanian armoured units in the Dothan Valley. This shows the aftermath, as Ouragon fighters harry the battered remnants of the Jordanian armour. (Peter Dennis © Osprey Publishing)

KHE SANH, JANUARY–JULY 1968

By the time the French left Indochina in 1956 the former French colony had been divided into North and South Vietnam. The north followed the Communist path established by Ho Chi Min, and south of the '17th Parallel' – the latitude of 17° North where it bisected Vietnam – a democratic government was established. The United States provided military aid to South Vietnam, as the country was subjected to a guerrilla campaign waged by the Viet Cong (VC), the Communist guerrilla movement active in South Vietnam. In 1964 President Johnson stepped up this military commitment, and by 1967 US forces were heavily involved in the campaign against the VC. By then, though, North Vietnam's People's Army of Vietnam

(PAVN) had been formed from the regular units of the Viet Minh, and were deployed in support of the VC guerrillas. During the early 1960s the South Vietnamese established combat bases in the remoter parts of the country, where they could prevent infiltration by VC or PAVN units. One of these, in the highlands of northern Quang Tri province near the 17th Parallel, was at Khe Sanh.

From 1966 on the PAVN had been moving PAVN and VC troops into the area, and late that year a small US Marine garrison was established at Khe Sanh to support the Army of the Republic of Vietnam (ARVN). The following April a PAVN division gathered to attack the base but was driven from the nearby hills by the 3rd Marine Regiment. Sporadic clashes continued, though, and by winter it was clear that the North Vietnamese were massing in numbers. Faced with the choice of whether to abandon the base or reinforce it, General Westmoreland, the senior US commander in Vietnam, decided to defend Khe Sanh, in the hope of luring the PAVN into a set-piece battle where their units could be destroyed. It was a similar situation to Dien Bien Phu, but the Americans had the advantage of massed airpower and helicopter mobility. The

LEFT As part of the Khe Sanh defences the Marines fortified the summits of a series of hills to the north of the base. In early 1968 these were assaulted by North Vietnamese regulars. In one attack on 6 February, the defences of Hill 861 were partially overrun before the PAVN could be driven back. (Peter Dennis © Osprey Publishing)

26th Marine Regiment was sent to Khe Sanh to defend the base and the outposts established on five of the hills overlooking it to the north.

The first clashes began in January and built in intensity, with regular PAVN artillery shelling of the base, and attacks on the outposts and on Khe Sanh village. American B-52 bombers pounded the surrounding jungle but this didn't prevent the PAVN from storming the nearby Special Forces base at Lang Vei on 7 February, where tanks were used to support the assault. The pressure on the hill outposts also increased, and it was now estimated that Khe Sanh was besieged by up to three PAVN divisions. By mid-March the situation was becoming critical, as more attacks were launched on the base perimeter.

The American response was to launch Operation *Pegasus*, an offensive by the 1st Air Cavalry Division to relieve Khe Sanh, in cooperation with US Marine units advancing on the base by road. The two-week operation was a success and inflicted significant casualties on the PAVN, as did further aggressive sweeps by the base's garrison. In all, over 4,000 PAVN troops were killed in the battle; however, it was now felt that Khe Sanh was untenable, so in late June and early July the base was abandoned. The Khe Sanh operation was indecisive, and many saw it as a pointless sacrifice of around 1,500 American lives, exposing the muddled thinking of senior US commanders.

HUE, 31 JANUARY–13 MARCH 1968

By January 1968 the American people were growing tired of America's commitment in Vietnam, with its continued toll of American lives. General Westmoreland, though, who commanded the American forces in Vietnam, assured President Johnson that his forces were winning what had become a war of attrition. He had no real idea that the North Vietnamese were planning a major offensive across the whole of South Vietnam. Early on 30 January the PAVN and VC launched simultaneous attacks in several South Vietnamese cities. Afterwards, this became known as the Tet Offensive. These involved sudden artillery bombardments on key points, followed by ground attacks. Most were dealt with by local troops, but the following night yet

more attacks were carried out all across the country, striking both towns and cities, including the capital Saigon, and also dozens of American army bases and airfields.

One of the cities attacked was Hue, an elegant and historic city on the Perfume River. Initial mortar attacks were followed by an assault by two PAVN regiments. Their target was the headquarters of the ARVN 1st Division situated in the Citadel, a square-shaped complex made up of the Imperial Palace and its gardens, ringed by a thick wall and a moat. Most of the Citadel was overrun, together with much of the city, but the headquarters staff managed to retain a foothold inside the historic complex. The Americans underestimated the strength of the PAVN there, and initially sent a single Marine company to recapture the city. By 1 February an ad hoc ARVN force made up of several units under Brigadier General Truong began to reclaim parts of the city.

General Westmoreland was slow to realize the scale of the problem, so it was another two days before a US Marine and US Army task group arrived from Phu Bai base to support Truong. By then the North Vietnamese defenders had fully entrenched themselves in the Citadel and six veteran battalions of VC did the same in the surrounding city. On 5 February, however, US Marines managed to fight their way through to the Citadel and gained a lodgement in its north-western corner. They lacked the firepower to advance further. Because of the historical and cultural significance of Hue, the Americans didn't use artillery and air strikes; instead they and the ARVN advanced street by street. Other American and South Vietnamese divisions surrounded the city, where they were engaged by more PAVN and VC units in the countryside.

However, in Hue itself the street clearing continued, and by 10 February the city south of the Perfume River had been recaptured. Three days later the Marines crossed the river on a hastily assembled pontoon bridge and reached the southern wall of the Citadel. It took another week to secure control of the southern gate, but now troops could be brought up for a final assault. Finally, on 24 February, ARVN troops fought their way into the Citadel, and recaptured the Imperial Palace complex. The following day the rest of the city was finally cleared. The bloody battle for Hue had cost over 3,700 US and ARVN casualties, and this more than anything exposed Westmoreland's claim that the war was being won. In fact, the reverse was more likely. It was also hugely costly for the PAVN and the VC, and the Tet Offensive was an enormous military setback for them. However, the political effect in terms of convincing the American people that the war was unwinnable had arguably been worth the sacrifice.

LEFT In the battle for Hue much of the Citadel was destroyed after it was turned into a fortress by its PAVN defenders. On 15–16 February a company of the 5th Marines finally captured the Dong Ba Gate, in the Citadel's north-eastern side, and so gained an entry point into the shattered complex. (Ramiro Bujeiro © Osprey Publishing)

THE SINAI, 14 OCTOBER 1973

After their victory in the Six Day War of 1967, the Israelis occupied the Sinai Peninsula, which ended on the eastern bank of the Suez Canal. Then, on 6 October 1973, the Egyptian Army launched a surprise assault across the canal and captured the Bar Lev defences, the Israeli fortifications guarding the eastern side of the canal. Then the Egyptian perimeter was advanced three miles into the desert to the east to protect Egyptian crossing points over the canal. The Israelis launched several counter-attacks to recapture their defences, but these were repulsed with heavy losses.

The Egyptians used Sagger anti-tank missiles (ATM) to defend their positions against Israeli tanks, while behind the canal massed Egyptian

surface-to-air missile (SAM) batteries prevented Israeli jets from supporting these assaults. In three days, the Israelis lost over 500 tanks. At the same time, heavy fighting was taking place between Israel and Syria on the Golan Heights, on the Israeli-Syrian border. This wider conflict became known as the Yom Kippur or October War. The Israelis were fighting on two fronts, and were unable to send sufficient reinforcements to the Sinai. However, Egyptian attempts to advance more than a few miles beyond the canal were thwarted by Israeli counter-attacks. Over 300 Egyptian tanks were destroyed, at negligible cost to the Israelis. After that, the Egyptians remained inside their bridgehead.

The situation had become a stalemate. This suited Egypt's President Sadat, though, as in any peace talks he could argue for the return of the Sinai. The Israelis, however, were eager for revenge. The stabilizing of the Golan front allowed them to move their reserves south, and by 14 October, after a series of poorly coordinated Egyptian armoured attacks were broken to the east of the Suez Canal, the Israelis were finally able to launch their counter-attack. The operation was organized by Major General Gonen, in charge of Israel's Southern Command.

Reconnaissance had revealed a gap in the Egyptian defences just north of The Great Bitter Lake, and this became the objective.

Three Israeli armoured divisions under Major Generals Adan, Sharon and Magen drove the Egyptians back, who were then pinned in place near the canal's east bank by Israeli mechanized units. This allowed an Israeli paratroop brigade to reach the eastern bank of the canal late on 15 October. That night Colonel Matt's paratroops crossed it in rubber boats to establish a bridgehead on the Egyptian side. A small armoured force followed, which attacked Egyptian SAM sites nearby. Realizing the gravity of this threat, the Egyptians launched an armoured counter-attack from the Sinai to the south of the crossing point, but this was repulsed by Adan's division and almost 200 Egyptian tanks were destroyed.

Meanwhile Israeli engineers had transported two pontoon bridges to the crossing point, and two days later these were in place. From 17 October onwards, the three Israeli armoured divisions crossed the canal and expanded the bridgehead as far as Ismailia and Suez. An entire Egyptian Army was now trapped on the wrong side of the canal, and Cairo, just 62 miles away, was wide open, so Egypt hurriedly arranged a UN-brokered ceasefire which was agreed on 25 October. After an initial disaster, the Israelis had completely reversed the military situation, and achieved one of the most spectacular victories in modern warfare.

DESERT STORM, 1991

In August 1990, the Iraqi Army invaded the tiny oil-rich state of Kuwait. Iraq's neighbour was conquered in just two days, amid widespread international protest. Saudi Arabia, fearing they would be next, appealed to their western allies for help. As a result, as the Iraqis dug in along Kuwait's southern border with Saudi Arabia, an international coalition was formed, led by the United States, but established under the banner of the United Nations. Its initial objective was to protect the Saudis in an operation codenamed *Desert Shield*. Over the months that followed considerable military forces were sent to Saudi Arabia, serving under an American commander, General Norman Schwarzkopf. By the end of the year a vast

armed camp had sprung up in the Saudi desert, with contingents assembled from 34 countries. Apart from the United States, the largest coalition force was fielded by Britain. Then in January 1991, after Iraq's President Saddam Hussein ignored a UN resolution demanding his withdrawal from Kuwait, Schwarzkopf was ordered to switch from a defensive posture to an offensive one. His new mission was to defeat the Iraqis, and liberate Kuwait.

In all, Schwarzkopf had over 700,000 personnel under his command, making him the commander of the largest military alliance since the end of World War II. His ground troops deployed behind the Saudi-Kuwaiti border were supported by coalition air forces equipped with the most modern equipment, including F-117 stealth aircraft, airborne early warning planes and powerful fighter-bombers. Equally impressive were the coalition naval forces deployed in the Persian Gulf. This invasion, codenamed Operation *Desert Storm*, was planned meticulously, and the troops were extensively trained. The invasion began on 17 January, with a four-week air bombardment of Iraqi defences and infrastructure. This operation, codenamed

Instant Thunder, resulted in civilian casualties, but it also caused the destruction of over 1,300 Iraqi tanks. An Iraqi attack on the Saudi coastal city of Khafji on 29 January was quickly repulsed.

On 24 February the ground offensive began, supported by a massed bombardment by 1,500 guns. The US VII and XIII Corps spearheaded the assault, initiating the largest tank battles for almost half a century around Norfolk and Medina Ridge. Within the first three days of the offensive over 1,000 Iraqi tanks had been destroyed, and the fighting potential of their Republican Guard destroyed. The British 1st Armoured Division cut off Kuwait City from the north, and the city was liberated by the US Marine Corps, and then the operation became a pursuit, the Iraqis hounded by incessant air attacks. By the time a ceasefire was declared on 28 January, VII Corps had advanced as far as the Euphrates valley. *Desert Storm* had been an outstanding success, won largely through superior military technology, supported by professional training and thorough planning. But political instability in the region remained a problem, and this eventually led to the far more controversial and costly Iraq War of 2003–11.

LEFT On 27 February, on the north flank of VII Corps advancing into northern Kuwait, the US 2-70 Armoured Battalion encountered the Iraqi 2nd Armoured Brigade on Medina Ridge. In the tank battle that followed the M-1 Abrams of 2-70 knocked out 59 Iraqi T-72s, without losing any tanks themselves. (Jim Laurier © Osprey Publishing)

OSPREY PUBLISHING
Bloomsbury Publishing Plc
Kemp House, Chawley Park, Cumnor Hill, Oxford OX2 9PH, UK
29 Earlsfort Terrace, Dublin 2, Ireland
1385 Broadway, 5th Floor, New York, NY 10018, USA
E-mail: info@ospreypublishing.com
www.ospreypublishing.com

OSPREY is a trademark of Osprey Publishing Ltd

First published in Great Britain in 2023

© Angus Konstam, 2023

Angus Konstam has asserted his right under the Copyright, Designs and Patents
Act, 1988, to be identified as Author of this work.

Artwork previously published in in the following Osprey titles: CAM 108:
Marathon 490 BC (p. 8); CAM 188: *Thermopylae 480 BC* (pp. 6–7, 10); CAM 222:
Salamis 480 BC (p. 12); CAM 239: *Plataea 479 BC* (p. 14); CAM 363: *Leuctra 371
BC* (p. 16); CAM 182: *Granicus 334 BC* (p. 18); CMD 11: *Hannibal* (back cover,
pp. 2, 20); CAM 299: *Zama 202 BC* (p.22); WPN 43: *The Composite Bow* (p. 24);
CAM 269: *Alesia 52 BC* (p. 26); CAM 174: *Pharsalus 48 BC* (p. 28); CAM 211:
Actium 31 BC (p. 30); CAM 228: *Teutoburg Forest AD 9* (p. 32); CAM 336:
Strasbourg AD 357 (p. 34); CAM 84: *Adrianople AD 378* (p. 36); CAM 286:
Catalaunian Fields AD 451 (p. 38); CAM 347: *Constantinople AD 717–18* (p. 42);
CAM 190: *Poitiers AD 732* (p. 44); ELI 9: *The Normans* (p. 46); CAM 262:
Manzikert 1071 (p. 48); CMD 12: *Saladin* (p. 50); CAM 46: *Lake Peipus 1242* (p.
52); CAM 217: *The Mongol Invasions of Japan 1274 and 1281* (p. 54); CAM 102:
Bannockburn 1314 (pp. 40–41; 56); CAM 332: *Kulikovo 1380* (front cover, p. 58);
CAM 122: *Tannenberg 1410* (p. 60); CMD 8: *Henry V* (p. 62); CAM 78:
Constantinople 1453 (p. 64); CAM 241: *The Fall of English France 1449–53* (p. 66);
CAM 360: *Bosworth 1485* (p. 68); CAM 321: *Tenochtitlan 1519–21* (p. 72); CAM
44: *Pavia 1525* (p. 74); CAM 372: *Cuzco 1536–37* (p. 76); CAM 50: *Malta 1565*
(p. 78); CAM 114: *Lepanto 1571* (p. 80); CAM 86: *The Armada Campaign 1588* (p.
82); CMD 24: *Tokugawa Ieyasu* (pp. 70–71, 84); CAM 170: *Osaka 1615* (p. 86);
CAM 68: *Lützen 1632* (p. 88); CAM 119: *Marston Moor 1644* (p. 90); CAM 191:
Vienna 1683 (p. 92); CAM 160: *Battle of the Boyne 1690* (p. 94); CAM 141:
Blenheim 1704 (p. 98); CAM 307: *Fontenoy 1745* (p. 100); CAM 113: *Rossbach and
Leuthen 1757* (pp. 102, 104); CAM 76: *Ticonderoga 1758* (p. 106); CAM 121:
Quebec 1759 (p. 108); CAM 67: *Saratoga 1777* (p. 110); CMD 21: *George
Washington* (pp. 96–97, 112); CAM 153: *Toulon 1793* (p. 116); CMD 16: *Horatio
Nelson* (pp. 118, 122); CAM 70: *Marengo 1800* (p. 120); CAM 191: *Vienna 1683*
(p. 124); WAR 24: *Austrian Grenadiers and Infantry 1788–1816* (p. 126); CAM 48:
Salamanca 1812 (p. 128); CAM 246: *Borodino 1812* (p. 130); CBT 4: *French
Guardsman vs Russian Jaeger* (p. 132); CAM 280: *Waterloo 1815 (3)* (p. 134); WPN
52: *Colt Single-Action Revolvers* (p. 138); CAM 207: *Solferino 1859* (p. 140); CMD
14: *Garibaldi* (p. 142); CBT 2: *Union Infantryman vs Confederate Infantryman* (pp.
136–137, 144); NVG 56: *Union River Ironclad 1861–65* (p. 146); CAM 374: *The
Battle of Gettysburg 1863 (1)* (p. 148); CAM 111: *Isandlwana 1879* (p. 150); CAM
57: *San Juan Hill 1898* (p. 152); CAM 330: *Tsushima 1905* (p. 154); CBT 11:
German Infantryman vs Russian Infantryman: 1914–15 (p. 158); CAM 221: *The
First Battle of the Marne 1914* (p. 160); WPN 41: *The Flamethrower* (p. 162); CAM
72: *Jutland 1916* (p. 164); CAM 169: *Somme 1 July 1916* (pp. 156–157, 166);
CAM 187: *Cambrai 1917* (p. 168); CAM 197: *Amiens 1918* (p. 170); CAM 349:
Warsaw 1920 (p. 172); CAM 264: *Fall Gelb 1940 (1)* (p. 176); ACM 1: *Battle of
Britain 1940* (p. 178); CAM 288: *Taranto 1940* (p. 180); CAN 167: *Moscow 1941*
(p. 182); CAM 62: *Pearl Harbor 1941* (p. 184); CAM 300: *Malaya and Singapore
1941–42* (p. 186); CAM 226: *Midway 1942* (p. 188); CAM 158: *El Alamein 1942*
(p. 190); WPN 23: *The M1903 Springfield Rifle* (pp. 174–175, 192); CAM 368:
Stalingrad 1942–43 (2) (p. 194); CMD 2: *Erich von Manstein* (p. 196); CAM 305:
Kursk 1943 (p. 198); CAM 229: *Kohima 1944* (p. 200); CAM 308: *St Lô 1944* (p.
202); CAM 370: *Leyte Gulf 1944 (1)* (p. 204); CAM 200: *Japan 1945* (p. 206);
CAM 162: *Inch'on 1950* (p. 210); CAM 366: *Dien Bien Phu 1954* (p. 212); CAM
216: *The Six Day War 1967* (p. 214); CAM 150: *Khe Sanh 1967–68* (p. 216); CAM
371: *The Battle of Hue 1968* (p. 218); CAM 126: *The Yom Kippur War (2)* (p. 220);
and DUE 18: *M1 Abrams vs T-72 Ural* (pp. 208–209, 222).

A catalogue record for this book is available from the British Library.

ISBN: HB 9781472856944;
eBook 9781472856951;
ePDF 9781472856920;
XML 9781472856937

23 24 25 26 27   10 9 8 7 6 5 4 3 2 1

Front cover artwork by Darren Tan © Osprey Publishing.
Back cover artwork by Peter Dennis © Osprey Publishing.
Cover, page design and layout by Stewart Larking
Originated by PDQ Digital Media Solutions, Bungay, UK
Printed in India through Replika Press Private Ltd.

Osprey Publishing supports the Woodland Trust, the UK's leading woodland
conservation charity.

To find out more about our authors and books visit www.ospreypublishing.com.
Here you will find extracts, author interviews, details of forthcoming events and the
option to sign up for our newsletter.